ED & ST~~ACIA CROWELL~~

We ♡
Re-Do

OUR JOURNEY TO
RECOMMITMENT & REDISCOVERY

ISBN: 978-1-716-32731-5

Produced by iWriteBooks Publishing
iWriteBooksPub.com

contents

PREFACE

DO I DO (STEVIE WONDER)

Like every couple starting out in love, we believed in "keeping yourself only to each other as long as you both shall live." Like too many couples, that was a vow we did not live up to.

The pain.

The anger.

The disbelief that this could happen to us.

The shame of being a *cheater*.

The hard work we knew lay ahead to repair our trust & relationship.

It almost took us out.

You know, many of us make inner vows to ourselves well before getting married. One of the most common one is: "I would *never* stay with someone who cheated on me." Especially because we saw infidelity in 'reference relationships' from our past, and hadn't dealt with the pain, it was one that both of us made well before meeting each other. We learned later, that making these types of vows are detrimental to our relationship with God and thus can be detrimental to our relationships with other people. After all, who are we to tell God that we are NOT going to allow Him to put us through a situation, if it is His will for us? Either to reveal something *to* us or to reveal something *through* us and bring us closer to Him. Reliance on Him, and *Him alone*, is the only way to survive certain circumstances in life. This is definitely that!

So how did we end up here? In a place where we are not just at peace with what almost destroyed us, but willing to tell the whole-wide world? "God made us do it!" Tell this story, that is. We've long heard, "You guys are the perfect couple," or "Do you guys *ever* fight?" Likely it is because our marriage of over 20 years has lasted longer than many others in this day and age and, no doubt, people would say things like this to us because we always seemed so happy. Side note: who goes putting their dirt on Facebook anyway? With a picture with red, puffy eyes, and a swollen nose from crying? Behind closed doors, there were years of our marriage when we were dying—even if we weren't honest with ourselves or each other about it.

What follows on these pages is a true love story, the song of our marriage, so each section will be titled with a song that we like. We amazingly have nearly identical musical tastes. We are a couple who have gone from the unbridled joy of being newlyweds, through the challenges of a new marriage with young children, and to the ultimate betrayal—infidelity, times two. Join us on a journey from distrust and total breakage, back to a seemingly impossible reconciliation, and a **Re-Do** on our marriage.

Let us be 100 with you, we were TERRIFIED to write this book and are still somewhat scared about what others' reactions will be. We were terrified because we hadn't even told our children what we had gone through, let alone the rest of our family or friends when we decided to write this book. Only a select few people knew, and we knew we'd have to sit down with our kids and tell them the whole ugly truth before this book ever saw the light of day. It's one thing to reveal to your kids your imperfections, but this was going to be a doozy! So many of us have been socialized to not put our personal business in the streets, yet God told us to trust Him. That He had a reason for all the pain we went through and that other couples would benefit from hearing our story. Hearing how self-centeredness, unrealistic expectations, and that we thought we were responsible for making each other happy instead of depending on Him, had us on the brink of filing those papers. But also, reading about how we threw our trust into God, even when we didn't feel like it, and found our way back.

You will hear the story from three sides:

Stacia's, "She-Do"

Ed's "He-Do"

Our common reflections and experiences, "We-Do".

Again, our goal in sharing our story is so that other couples can see how a happy union can go wrong. Quickly. And to ANYONE. We want readers to be on the lookout for unresolved pain, circumstances and yes, even other people that could derail a marriage, and fight *for* each other instead of fighting *with* each other. While there is no 'secret sauce', the following learning lessons can help couples hold their relationship together if it's in trouble, and also keep healthy couples on the right track. We'll get to those after we spill the tea. We've chosen certain songs to help us do that and have curated a Spotify playlist to accompany our story as sometimes music speaks to the soul in a way that mere words cannot. You'll see just how eclectic our musical taste can be!

The public Spotify list is called **We Re-Do**. Scan our QR Code on the next page for quick access and to be taken directly to the playlist.

We stumbled, and fumbled, our way back to each other, and looking back, God ordered every single one of those steps. Even when we couldn't feel Him. Even when we were outwardly MAD at him for letting our marriage deteriorate to such a place.

CHAPTER 1

She-Do:

PUBLIC SERVICE ANNOUNCEMENT (JAY-Z)

Allow me to (re)introduce myself, my name is Stacia (Hall) Gowens. I grew up in the East Lansing / Lansing Michigan area. I was blessed to have a very loving family, many diverse, and close friends, exposure to athletics, performing arts, a solid education, and just an all-around strong upbringing. I was blessed culture that is vastly available when you live in a college town, hard-working and educated parents, aunts, uncles, and grandparents! I remember a lot of good times; (translation: parties, parties and more parties). At the high-school I graduated from, J.W. Sexton High School (you should've been a Big Red), we would create flyers for house parties and many were hosted at local union halls in the Lansing area.

In time though, my childhood was marred by the separation and eventual divorce of my parents. Now, I am not going to tell all of *their* business, but I can say, as the oldest sibling (my only blood-sister is 8.5 years younger than me), I really felt I needed to hold it all together. Be strong and figure out this whole *two separate households* thing for the both of us. Being a tween-ager, I thought I did a good job. When my Dad told me he was remarrying, I got out of his car and just ran into the open field where he was building his house to share with my stepmom and step-sister. I think I saw that in a movie or after school special, ha-ha. I thought it was what I was *supposed* to do! In hindsight, I internalized much of their failed marriage into my view of, and ultimately, the handling of my own marriage.

The dissolution of their union, as well as "feminist-correct" societal norms, led me to unknowingly create Capital "V" vows that I would NEVER let my marriage end in divorce. In fact, I had developed a long list of "nevers" for my marriage.

What 'feminist-correct' norms am I talking about?

1) I would never let my husband be the sole breadwinner. I noted and modeled my strong, smart, capable mother as she continued to handle everything thrown her way after her divorce because she had enabled herself to stand on her own two-feet financially. I earned both a bachelor's and a master's degree in marketing, so that I would be able to do the same.

2) I would never tolerate my husband not communicating with me—and with the quickness! If I asked a question and there was not a response in what I deemed to be a timely fashion, there was hell to pay.

3) I would never, not ever, stay with an unfaithful man. Period. Point Blank. Do NOT pass Go. Do NOT collect $200.

Of course, I am not saying having standards for how someone treats you are in a relationship with is a bad thing. *In fact, it's advisable.* But a standard and a VOW are two different things and, I would learn much later at our church home in Texas, One Community Church (Dr. Conway Edwards, Lead Pastor), that making a vow is an act of disobedience against God. I mean, who am I (and who are you) to tell God what you won't allow him to take you through? How arrogant to think that we are so important that we deserve *nothing* but sunshine and smooth sailing for our whole lives when Jesus suffered a great deal for us?

The focus of American society, indeed many Western societies, in the 20th and 21st centuries has been on happiness. The truth of the matter is, if we have the wonderful blessing of being happy for 80% of our lives, we should be thanking our lucky stars and our heavenly Father (if you are a Christian, Allah, Buddha, your higher power - you get the point). A person's true character is revealed during tough times. When things absolutely go the opposite of their way, how do they react? Do they calmly consider their faith and quickly forgive someone who does them wrong? NOT!

In high school and college, I had a couple of serious boyfriends—but I was certainly too young to think seriously about marriage. In fact, during my third year of college, I began working as a student aide in the Office of the President of Michigan State University. The Hannah Administration Building didn't have a real cafeteria, more like an old office converted into a convenient store of sorts. One day, I was needing some brain food and I happened to run into this "older" guy that I had seen before and reminded me of another guy I briefly dated Freshman year (so that is to say - I thought he was good looking). He worked for the Administrative Information

Systems department on the bottom floor of the building and he must have had the same afternoon munchies. I peeked around him to see what he was buying and remarked that his choice of Funyuns and peanut butter cookie, "sure looks healthy," and then I disappeared out of the store and back to my office. I didn't see the guy again until....

Fast forward to the Fall of my fifth year at Michigan State University (#GoGreen). Graduation was so close I could taste it and I had just completed a successful internship with Armstrong World Industries in Lancaster, PA. I knew I had done a good job because I received an offer for full-time employment after receiving my Bachelor of Arts in Marketing and was full of excitement about all of the promises of my soon-to-be "grown-up life".

And then it happened. One morning I was headed to work from the parking garage, earlier than normal. All of a sudden I saw someone in my periphery and heard a man say, "Hey, I see you all of the time. What is your name?" That's it. That's the pick-up line that ultimately hooked me. I told him my name and asked him for his. Edward Gowens. That's about all the time we spent talking to each other that morning before going separate directions on the elevator.

This is one time when the office grapevine worked for the greater good! I had mentioned my interest in "the guy down in AIS" to my boss, Theresa Pharms, who was good friends with a woman in AIS. I admit, I was kind of sad when Theresa learned that he was married, but I quickly put him out of my mind. A few weeks later, as Ed was talking with some of his colleagues, someone mentioned that a "girl from the fourth floor" had been asking about him—but that another coworker said that he was married. Ed exclaimed, "I'm not married! That's Kevin. The *other* Black guy!"

While I was upstairs a little sad that I missed my chance, Ed was downstairs, writing me a note to set the record straight.

He planned to hand-deliver the note to the fourth floor at lunchtime, figuring I would be in class and he could make a quick retreat without risking possible face-to-face rejection. But as fate would have it, there I sat. At the front desk. What would he do?

He-Do:

HI! MY NAME IS... (EMINEM)

No—not Slim Shady—though he *is* from the D (Detroit) like I am.

I was born on the eastside of Detroit, in 1968 at Hutzel hospital, in the year of turmoil that contained the assassinations of MLK and Robert F Kennedy. My mother had moved from Pickens, South Carolina with my Aunt Johnnie, and lived a short distance from my other Aunt, Nancy. It was while she was attending Wayne State University that she met my father, and after a short courtship, I popped up onto the scene. My father was *only* separated from his wife at the time my mother became pregnant, so needless to say my mom's pregnancy made everything...let's just say complicated.

My mother went back to school to finish her degree but needed help with me. Through a family friend, she met two ladies, Mrs. Hall and Ms. Parsha, who agreed to help babysit me while she attended classes. Even though they were of no relation to me, they immediately grew attached to me (and I to them), and they became my de facto godparents. So, with a majority of my mom's side of the family still in the south, and the fact that I had little contact with my father and his side of the family, these two ladies became influential factors in my life outside of my mom and my two aunts.

After my mother finished her education and had worked several jobs, she and my Aunt Johnnie decided to take a leap of faith and move to California to escape the harsh winters of the Midwest, and to improve their financial situation on the west coast. I had initially started kindergarten in Detroit, but once we made the move to California, I would start my elementary schooling in Los Angeles at Hobart Elementary. We lived in an area of LA that was streaming with diversity (now called Koreatown) and my childhood memories were filled with every nationality of friends from Japanese, Korean, Mexican, Guatemalan, Panamanian, and just a sprinkling of white folks here and there.

Now, during this time I still visited "The D" (what we *real* Detroiters affectionately call our city) occasionally and would also travel to South Carolina to stay connected with my mom's side of the family. I would visit with my grandmother and her mother, my uncles, and a host of cousins and family friends. As I finished elementary school, my mom began to increasingly struggle with mental health issues, and for a while, it was very difficult for me to discern what was happening and understand her diagnosis—bipolar disorder and schizophrenia. Eventually, I would leave LA to spend a summer with my grandmother (and great-grandmother), which turned into a formal move to Pickens, S.C. I would live there for two years as my mom tried to deal with her illness, which included various misdiagnoses, treatments, and the hardships from the economic challenges of the late '70s and early '80s.

Living in Pickens compared to LA was like comparing the television show "Beverly Hills 90120" to the movie "Mad Max: Beyond Thunderdome." To put it in perspective, I was a pre-teen moving from a diverse city of sun and fun, to the simple countrified living of a small southern town still grappling with the unraveling of segregation, racial inequality, and integration all at the same time! Needless to say, it was one thing to visit this part of the country and a completely different thing to live and breathe this new reality.

Following my stint in Pickens, I found myself back in "The D" in the summer of '81, visiting with my godparents (Big Mama, Mr. Hall, and Ms. Parsha). It was like I had been paroled from the "Land of the Lost," but then was thrown into the movie "Cooley High." The original plan was for me to visit with my godparents, and also my Aunt Nancy and great-uncle who were still in Detroit, for the summer and then return to LA with my mom. But I soon learned that my mom was having increasingly more challenges in managing her illness, and she, along with my Aunt Johnnie recommended I stay in Detroit and start middle school there.

Through it all, I was able to survive these challenges and went from a reserved and introverted high schooler to graduating from Jared W. Finney high school in 1986 as Summa Cum Laude, Senior Class Vice-President, Vice-President of the National Honor Society, with acceptance letters from a host of colleges. The next chapter of my life started when I decided to attend Michigan State University and major in engineering, which began my journey into manhood.

There are certain special moments in life that you never forget like a first kiss, your most embarrassing moment from high school, and your first love. I thought on a couple of occasions that I had met the "woman of my dreams," but truthfully, I was mistaken each time. When I finally met my wife, I can honestly say there was a definite attraction, but I would not immediately know for sure if she was going to be *the one*. I mean, I didn't immediately go there after the interaction Stacia described; when she issued the not-so-subtle dig about the nutritional content of my Funyuns and peanut butter cookie.

I do have to give a special shout out to my best friend who happened to work with me in the IT department on MSU's campus. It was he who would continuously nudge me to "say something" to that "pretty young thang" we had peeped on numerous occasions in the MSU administration building. Our "official" initial contact was very fortuitous, so much so that I could not remember her name after she shared it with me. As mentioned, we happened to work in the same building on campus and would pass each other semi-regularly in the hallways of the administration building. Immediately, I noticed her smile and how her face lit up as our eyes met and as we gave each other the universal black person head nod for "I see you my brother/sister." Occasionally I would let a "Hey, you" slip out, or, "How you doin'" (in my Joey Tribiani, voice).

I always thought it was odd that our paths kept crossing, yet we couldn't get past the friendly wave and smile at one another. Looking back on it, I imagine this was God putting her in my path and saying to me in a whisper, "Go ahead, introduce yourself!" But true-to-form, as I am much more reserved than most guys, I chose the path of least resistance by doing the least to engage her and ignored that push to just go for it.

That is until one morning on my way into my job, I was leaving the parking structure by the administration building and I noticed her about 10 yards in front of me. Instantly, I had this rush of angst that came over me and some type of supernatural push that sped me up until I was right behind her. I took a deep breath, cleared my throat, and said, "Hey you, good morning." Immediately, I got the bubble guts, and felt as though I was going to crap my pants! She turned my way and smiled, and with that my heart melted. I don't remember what she said, but I seemed to mutter something about who I was, my name, and it was good to finally speak to her. She told me her name and we chatted all the way to the door of the building where she went left, and I went right.

Stasha. Wait, Stay-Sha. No, that's not it. Stacey? Ugh. I just gained some cool points in my mind by engaging her in our first real interaction, and now I'm struggling to remember her name. I just met her and can't even get her name right. Ok, it's something like Stacie or whatever. The point is, I got the name. Now, I'll work on being more engaging, show her my little swagger, and then I'll ask for the digits.

Quick pause for those of you who are not familiar with getting "the digits." See, back in the 80s and 90s that was slang for getting her phone number. Her home number! No one had mobile phones back then, and you had to hope that they had an answering machine if the person didn't pick up the phone. However, in this case, I never saw Stacia again. I mean, she disappeared from campus and I assumed from the world! Damn. I missed my chance to connect and I thought to myself that I should have been brave enough to score those digits right then. Lesson learned, never put off doing something right away.

Now, unbeknownst to me, a co-worker of mine and a co-worker of hers inadvertently had conversations about us, and due to nothing short of a miracle, our paths were put on a course to intersect again. First things first, I had to find a way to quickly intercede when inaccurate information was shared with her about my relationship status. You have already heard from Stacia that she was told I was married, and I knew immediately I had to grow some cojones and fix this. I found out what office and floor she worked on and I ran up four flights of steps to her office, and she's right, I hoped she wouldn't be there, so I could drop a note and run. Instead, I sucked it up, re-introduced myself, and gave her *my digits*! As I walked away and headed down to my office, after talking to her for literally an hour, doubt and apprehension crept into my head. I felt like I just lost all kinds of cool points by looking desperate. But thank goodness for fate and God's design, because she called me that day and we've been in each other's lives ever since. Of course, the story of *us* was just beginning.

We-Do:
LOVE AT FIRST SIGHT (MARY J BLIGE & METHOD MAN)

So, it was practically love at first conversation, at least that's what it felt like. The truth is, you can fall in 'like' with someone after one conversation. You can fall in 'lust' with someone with no conversation at all.

Love—while it is a splendid thing—takes really getting to know someone; the good, the bad, the ugly, and the very-*very* ugly. We subscribe to the notion that love is not a feeling, it is a choice.

When times get tough relationally, you have to *choose to love*.

When the financial picture looks bleak, you have to *choose love*.

When you disagree about child-rearing, *love is the way*.

Even when one spouse shatters the other's heart, they both have to *choose love*.

So, while we certainly seemed to click early on and enjoyed each other's company, falling in love would take much more than their perfect first date in October of 1994 at Crunchy's, an East Lansing burger hotspot.

For example, Stacia's parents were divorced and Ed's were never married. There is a certain amount of trauma that comes with that and if we had didn't deal with these issues before vowing to become one, there were obstacles we were bound to run into and be ill-equipped to handle.

What about communication? Ed learned early on in life not to upset the apple cart because, with his mother's mental health conditions, if she were set off, it could mean them losing their basic living arrangements. Stacia, on the other hand, living with all women, would fuss and yell and slam doors all the time as a regular method of (okay, yes, ineffective) communication. How would those two styles work together? Spoiler alert: Not very well.

Fortunately, the one thing we had on our side was that we did like each other. Truly and genuinely so that seemed to be enough, at least early on, to keep us together and moving forward. We, of course, learned later in our relationship that not dealing with issues openly can lead to very toxic outcomes.

What do you need?

If YOU can't articulate what you need—not want—need, then THEY have no chance in coming close to meeting them. During one of our very first marriage counseling sessions, our homework assignment was to write down our top ten needs in a relationship. Oh. Em. Gee! This was exceptionally hard for Stacia! In fact, even when the therapist was giving the assignment, and the word, *need* came out of her mouth, Stacia says she started sweating. She had a physiological response to just the word *need*. She even called her best friend afterward and droned on and on about how ridiculous it was and that she didn't NEED anyone! While it's true that we shouldn't expect any human, including our betrothed, to make us happy, this assignment wasn't that. This was more along the lines of need:

To know that the other person **believes** in them

To be **respected**

To feel **safe**

To be **listened** to

To know they are **understood** and **appreciated** (and not that they need to think, behave as the other person does)

To know they can **trust** their spouse

To know that nothing was too hard to talk about and resolve

To have true companionship/**friendship**

Spiritual intimacy and alignment

To feel peace and tranquility in the relationship

For this marriage to work, it was going to take individual and collective reflection on their history, hang-ups and norms, honesty, vulnerability, and much more. In reality, this is more than anyone, including Ed and Stacia, truly bargains for when they say I do!

CHAPTER 2

She-Do:

YOUNG LOVE (JANET JACKSON)

In the Fall of 1994, I was in my last semester at Michigan State and was excited about my new job with Armstrong World Industries. Armstrong is based in the heart of Amish country, Lancaster, PA, and I was assigned the sales territory that covered almost the entire state of Pennsylvania, as well as New Jersey and Delaware. Ed and I started dating exclusively right away and so in one of our first conversations, I shared that I was excited about my new job, that I would be moving to Pennsylvania and that I was *not* interested in a long-distance relationship! I told him, he didn't have to move to PA, but I was, and I wasn't dating him in Michigan. Now, I had done the distance relationship thing and was not at all interested in ever doing that again! That was but one of my experiences being cheated on and, not surprisingly, I wasn't eager to repeat that experience.

Maybe that's why our exclusive status was a point that I felt I had to make clear to a couple of his exes early on (something that I didn't identify as insecurity, and he didn't identify as "these chicks really are pushing up on me"). For example, very early on in the relationship, Ed caught the chickenpox at 26 years old. Now, to the ladies reading this book, you know how it is when love is new, and you are turning on the "best woman in the world" charm full tilt? I went to his apartment to bring him some soup and sit with him for a while and when I got there, his friend - a female friend - was leaving. I think we exchanged quick hellos in the hallway in passing and of course, my Inspector Gadget came right on out.

Me: "Who was that?"

Him: "Oh just my friend Taylor (name changed to protect the guilty)

Me: "OK" (please read this making the face you imagine I was making at the time)

Only later did I find out that Taylor was his ex-girlfriend. Bringing my *current* boyfriend soup, not cool! If my recollection is correct, I didn't fly off the handle, which would've been my normal MO. Remember, this relationship was still new, I wasn't trying to scare him off. But that would be the first of many times I had to explain women to him. Sometimes we can be conniving, manipulative, fickle, selfish; facts that other women are constantly tuned into, whereas men, well, just ain't!

When I did find out, I admonished him for not telling me the truth the first time (I mean, he must've known I'd have a problem if he didn't reveal her ex status the first time) and I tried to put him up on game. For those of you not familiar with that slang phrase, Urban Dictionary defines 'put you up on game' as: 1) To tell someone new or uninformed how to survive in their environment who to respect, who to get over on, and overall how to win; 2) To tell you how it is and how it will be. Simply put, taking care of you when you are sick is your woman's job—and *only* your woman's job—unless we are talking about your Mother!

She knew that, and I knew she knew that.

This was her trying to weasel her way back in. I know he felt I was overreacting, and I knew he was being naive. If he didn't know it at the time, Ed was beginning to understand that he had fallen for a very headstrong young woman who had no issues sharing her point of view. Looking back, if we had been mature enough and had been playing close enough attention, we would've communicated about this first red flag very differently and may not have found ourselves, letting the lines get crossed over and over again which was a factor that led to the betrayal(s).

The next early hiccup came when I told my beloved Aunt Debbie (RIP - miss you every day), that I thought something must be seriously wrong with this guy. I said, "I think I have to break up with him. I mean, he's nice to me. He writes me poetry. He has an apartment and a car that are both clean and he pays for them on time. He cooks. He even has a little money in the bank. WHY wouldn't he be married at 26 years old?" I was only 23 at the time and I thought that everyone married in their mid-20s so what was wrong with this dude? Then I dropped the bomb, "He's either a serial killer, *or* he's gay!" Let me tell you, I was the first child born in our family, first niece, first grandchild, first everything so to say that my family always treated me as special is an understatement. They always had my back...a real Stacie and fam vs. Everybody vibe (side note: I didn't like Stacia growing up because no one could pronounce it, so to this day this is what my family calls me—even though they all seem to spell it differently).

Now, my Aunt who stood all of 4 feet 9 inches tall looked up at me. Pointed her finger in my face, and said, "What are you talking about? DON'T YOU MESS THIS UP!"

Wow. What are you sayin—I'm your niece, your first baby—you just met this Gowens cat and you are telling me that I would be messing up by breaking up with him? Well, I trusted my Auntie. She was tough and strong and saw something in Ed that made her immediately protective. So needless to say, I put the thought of breaking up with him out of my mind. He was officially, "my guy."

Other than those two blips on the relationship radar, I'd say our getting along was quite easy. We had the same sense of humor, enjoyed the same music, movies, other forms of entertainment, the whole nine. And after a little while, he decided that he would look for a job in Pennsylvania. He was willing to give up the life he was building for himself (albeit in my hometown of Lansing which was a great place to grow up, but not all that hard to leave as an adult—LOL).

He-Do:
LOVE THANG (INTRO)

Now, before Stacia, I was living the single life in a college town where a typical day was work, then hanging with a few friends on the weekends. Occasionally, I would still travel to The D for a little escape from the small city feel of East Lansing.

Dating during this time was like being at the grocery store and shopping for fresh fruit. I'd spend time first looking over the choices, then picking an item up and then quickly placing it back as if the color and texture felt all wrong. Then for those pieces of fruit that peaked my attention, I'd hold them, squeeze them, and maybe sample them. But eventually, I'd end up putting them back and moving on, feeling empty and unsatisfied. But once Stacia and I began to get serious and spend more time together, I was nervously ready to admit that I had met the one.

The following lyrics from the R&B group Intro's song, Love Thang, sums up my feelings for Stacia:

Honey don't you know that I been waiting, every day anticipating

For a woman just like you to come my way

I been searching the right and wrong til I'm so glad you came along

To end this loneliness I found

And it's good to have you around

I was drawn to her beauty, her confidence, and self-determination. She had the entire package that I desired; from her sense of humor, her sex appeal, to her intelligence. And she had way more style and cool points than me. We were firing on all cylinders as we began to spend more time with one another, and I soon began to focus on making sure I didn't mess this thing up because I had never had this exact connection before. Looking back, I realize this need to "not rock the boat" would be detrimental to our relationship and would lead us down a path that would break both of us.

In the meantime, we had nothing but bright and sunny days. There were cute moments like having our first date at Crunchy's. I was introduced to her immediate family who lived in the Lansing area, including several cousins who were basically like her siblings as they were and are a close-knit group. When I initially met her mom and sister, I could immediately tell this was a close-knit family who loved hard and played hard, which made me feel as though I had jumped into a mash-up between The Cosby Show, Martin, and Family Matters. I also relish that funny moment early on in our relationship when her dear Aunt Debbie quipped, "Girl, he is a good man! You better not blow it!" We owe her big time for saving our relationship because Stacia was ready to jump ship; all because a brother could cook a mean pork chop and made his bed, she thought something had to be amiss.

Now meeting her father for the first time was similar to one of my favorite movies, "Meet the Parents". I was the character Greg, played by Ben Stiller and her father was Mr. Burns, played by the incomparable Robert DeNiro. Her father was in law enforcement (just like Jack Burns) and was a no-nonsense type of guy with a serious scowl on his face (also, just like Jack Burns). Stacia did nothing to help calm my nerves as she used this opportunity to instill fear in me about how her father likes to have conversations with boyfriends out back, all the way by "The Tree". I never saw this tree and I had no desire to see the said tree. I had no clue if Stacia was pulling my leg or if she was trying to see if she could punk me!

What I did know is that I needed to be on my best behavior and say nothing to make this man want to pull out his gun and shoot me in the face. Of course, looking back on this, I should have known it was a ruse by both of them to have a little fun at my expense.

As Stacia has already said, she had secured a permanent job in Pennsylvania, following graduation. Now, we disagree on exactly how the decision was made that I would move from Michigan to live with her in Pennsylvania, *my* recollection of the conversation went along the lines of her telling me that she had a job already lined up in Pennsylvania and that she didn't do long-distance relationships. This was followed by a deadpan facial expression with her head slightly cocked to the side as if to indicate I better say the right thing. This was my chance to hit that perfect pitch out of the park, so my response was, "I'm coming with you, of course!" Later on, we would realize that this was our first step in learning to depend on each other - as we would be walking away from the comfort of living around lots of friends and family and establish who we were as a couple.

We-Do:
FALLIN' (ALICIA KEYS)

Love was young and new, and we had fallen for each other. Looking back, as is the case with most couples, in the beginning, there was a certain amount of 'agency' going on - meaning we weren't dating each other's real selves, we were dating each other's agents. We both tried hard to be on our very best behavior and not to offend the other for fear of the relationship ending before it got good and started. The truth is, we still had a lot to learn about each other, not least of which was to have clear and honest conversations.

Be clear in communication and watch your timing.

We didn't seem to have a problem communicating simple information to each other, but when it came to difficult conversations, we avoided those like the plague. We rarely got to the root of any issue. Remember the "Taylor thing" when Ed had an ex-girlfriend hanging around? Having the guts to dive deep with Stacia on how the incident made her feel, and why, he could've avoided contributing to her insecurities in the future and avoided being seen as being emotionally inept or worse, not considerate of her feelings. He can admit now that he handled our early issues like most men, which is to have a conversation, everyone then states their case, and then we throw that mug into the "sea-of-forgetfulness" and never bring that issue up again. The first marriage counselor we went to helped him see why that never works with women, using language he, as an IT professional, can understand. "Women are like PCs. You may be working in one window, but there are about 20 windows open in the background." There is no sea of forgetfulness for women. Unless you have the right communication skills as a man, you won't get to the real issue so that she is willing to close that particular window to deal with the other windows running in the background.

Mind the HOW as well as the WHAT

Stacia admits that she really hadn't learned how to communicate when she was upset, in a way that wasn't, well, let's call it what it was, flying off the handle. In hindsight (which is clear as a mug), she should've taken the time to consider how her message was being relayed. Yelling, slamming doors, driving off in great haste, served absolutely zero purpose in ever actual communication and was tuned out by Ed who, as discussed, grew up in an environment where volatility could literally be the difference between living in a home or a shelter. It also served to teach Ed that he may as well keep any difficult conversations to himself, less he invoked Stacia's wrath.

We could have avoided much of what we would later put each other through if we had only been mature enough to talk through issues even when they were difficult. Instead, we called ourselves "letting it go," or "moving on," when we were clearly not solving problems that ended up catching up to us.

chapter 3

She-Do:

MOTOWNPHILLY (BOYZ II MEN)

In May of 1995, I walked across that stage and received my Bachelor of Arts Degree in Marketing and the event was made oh so special as President William Jefferson Clinton was our Commencement speaker and my Papa missed the Kentucky Derby for the first time—like ever! It was such a magical time, I was at the real jumping-off place of adulthood. I recall telling my Mother that Ed was planning to move to Philadelphia and that we were moving in together. She was apprehensive about this at first and asked, "What if you meet another man out there? I mean - aren't you shooting yourself in the foot?" My response came swiftly, "It will be mighty hard to meet someone else when I LIVE with my boyfriend!" I have always been a bit of a smart aleck.

My adulting adventure would be with Ed by my side, as he agreed (or relented - not quite sure which it was) to move to

Philadelphia with me! The condition that he put on his moving ½ way across the country with me, was that he had to find a job first, not a bad condition to have. He has always been a man who understands his role as a provider, never a moocher.

The orientation for new employees began in June and my company provided temporary housing for a month until I could secure a place of residence. Back then, many large companies provided full relocation assistance, so in addition to temporary housing, they packed all of my belongings, including my car, and prepared to move them to Philadelphia.

Now, Ed hadn't yet secured a job yet, but was scheduled for a few interviews and was in the process with about three different companies. He would visit me a couple of times during his interviews - and in his mind, if he didn't find a position soon, it must mean that we were not meant to be. He didn't actually communicate that to me at the time, but our relationship was 'on the clock', and time was ticking away.

Fortunately, he was offered an opportunity with a small consulting company just as his internal deadline approached. He packed up, ended his lease, secured housing for his Mother (who had unexpectedly moved into his apartment earlier in the year) and set off on the drive from Michigan to Pennsylvania, a nine-and-a-half-hour trip, with him and his best friend trading off driving time through the winding mountains of Pennsylvania!

I was beyond thrilled that he was with me now, and hopefully *forever*. I'd been in committed relationships before, but this one felt different from the word go. We found a nice little one-bedroom apartment with a den on American Way in King of Prussia, PA, and had all of my belongings delivered. We added my few articles of furniture to what Ed brought from his apartment. As a matter of fact, except for the water bed (yes, I had a waterbed and moved that sucker all the way to Pennsylvania), almost all of the furniture was his.

This included his beloved Papasan chair, he loved that chair! It only survived the move to Pennsylvania but quickly became a casualty of my decorating style vs. Ed's.

At first, living together was a breeze. We joked when I found his high school track letterman's sweater in the closet and it had "The Ace" embroidered on the back and I asked why in the world HIS letterman's sweater bore MY nickname? We'd had the same nickname in high school - it must be meant to be! Once I found some communications about old flings of his and we had a fight about it, too. Was he still pining for these women who were no more than casual flings? Or was he getting bored with being in a monogamous relationship and I should be prepared for the inevitable, him moving on? Whatever his answers were to why he was maintaining this correspondence, they weren't satisfactory to me at the time, but I tried to push down my feelings of discomfort and move forward in the relationship. This is never a good idea. If one of the partner's feelings are not fully explored and resolved, the problem will continue to pop its head into the relationship at best and lead to destruction at worst.

After living together for several months, in December of 1995, Ed popped THE question. Now, this wasn't a complete surprise, we had gone ring shopping and Ed had me choose my engagement ring because he didn't want to get this one wrong. It makes sense, we had only been dating for a little over a year. Even though we were very close and together all of the time, how well do you know someone's taste in jewelry in such a short time? How do you know anything about someone in a year, LOL? I am sure our friends and family thought this was a very quick engagement, of course, they were right, but we believed we were ready–we had found *the one* in each other.

So, getting to the engagement story, because it is classic. Classic me! As I mentioned, it was December and Ed told me about his company's Christmas party and that all team members and their significant others were invited. I thought, "How great! I'll get to meet some of his co-workers." It was being hosted at a fancy French restaurant, so when the day came, I relished getting all dolled up for the experience. When we arrived at the restaurant, I noted we were at least thirty minutes early for the event. As Ed put the car into park, I quickly stated that, since we had time, I wanted to go to the Gap which was located in the same shopping area as the restaurant, because there were a few Christmas gifts I had yet to purchase. Ed looked at me and in a very uncharacteristic way, barked, "NO" at me, and promptly got out of the car and closed the door. I gasped. *The gall. The nerve.* First of all, I thought to myself, you are *not* the boss of me and if I want to go to the Gap first, before your little funky Christmas party (see how quickly I went from being excited, to thinking it was a "funky lil' Christmas party") I most certainly will! He just stood there. Outside of the car on the driver's side. I would find out later why he didn't even come to my side of the car to open my door but started to head toward the restaurant. After picking my jaw up off of the ground and saying aloud to myself, "This dude must be crazy," I got out of the car and walked toward the restaurant as well.

Once inside the restaurant, Ed could tell that I had a big ole attitude about what just went down at the car, and he was actively avoiding any conversation about it. Just as I began thinking, I don't even want to be here with him, the host returned and informed us that our party hadn't arrived yet, but he could seat us at a table while we waited. How dumb, I thought. Why would we sit at a table vs. at the bar or where we stood if we were waiting only twenty minutes or so to go upstairs where the party was being held?

After we were seated, he must've struck up an attempt at some small talk while I continued steaming about what had just happened. We ordered drinks and appetizers when he announced to me that maybe the party was postponed because no one was there. He didn't work for some rinky-dink operation, so this didn't sound right to me, but when he suggested we move forward and order entrees, I didn't protest because, frankly, I was annoyed and wanted to just eat and go home. Then he proceeded to tell the waiter to go ahead and bring our entrees. Wait a minute. How does he know what we want, we never ordered? What the heck was going on with this guy, I thought. He had never behaved like this before.

Our meals arrived rather quickly and they both were covered with those heavy silver domes and I immediately thought *lobster*! There must be a whole lobster underneath that thing! When the waiter removed the dome from my plate first, he revealed my engagement ring. It took me several breaths to figure out what was happening. That's my ring. That's my ring. THAT'S MY RING...oh my goodness, this is it!

Remember how I mentioned he wrote me beautiful poems early in our relationship? He got down on one knee and recited a "will you be my wife" poem! Without hesitation, I answered *yes,* and the room erupted in applause! He had made me the happiest girl in the world, and I think I repaid that favor. It took about 15 minutes, after our waiter brought our actual meals, that I exclaimed, "Wait a minute! There is no company holiday party, is there?" This was a night to remember and I was so excited about getting right to the planning for the day I would become Mrs. Stacia Hall-Gowens (I was stuck on hyphenating my name at the time as my dad has only daughters. It lasted about six months).

We were married in my childhood church in front of about 200 family and friends on October 5, 1996. At the time we thought our ceremony was awesome, but when we watch the video all these years later, we wonder why we subjected our guests to all of that, LOL. It was at least an hour and a half too long.

Settling back into our newlywed life in Pennsylvania was great. Ed couldn't wait to get me to the bank, to the Department of Motor Vehicles, the Social Security office, and anywhere else my last name would need to be changed! A few months after getting married, we discussed whether and when we would consider expanding our new family. While Ed wanted to wait, "until we could afford a child" I exclaimed we would never be able to afford them and because I was the one that had to cook 'em and push 'em out, I wanted to start sooner rather than later.

Well, it seemed no sooner than I stopped taking birth control pills, we found out we were pregnant with our first child. The only thing I know is that he was conceived after we were married (a fact I remember having to calculate, because when we told our church family at Mt. Zion AME Church, Devon, PA, they automatically started doing the math in their heads).

Ed knew how much I wanted a house when our son arrived, instead of living in a one-bedroom with an office, so he took on a second job working for a small marketing firm, selling MBNA MasterCards over the phone. Yes, he was one of the people that others yelled at for interrupting their dinner to hock credit cards, but he was on a mission to provide a home for his wife and his soon-to-be-born child. And I was so grateful when we bought our first house in Limerick, PA. I mention the city because the only thing in Limerick at the time was a nuclear power plant, but it was affordable, new construction, and we were so proud of that house!

Christopher Jonathan Gowens, my beautiful boy, was born one week before our first anniversary, September 28, 1997. Since this book has a musical vibe, let me mention that I *love* Earth Wind and Fire (got it from my daddy and passed it on to Chris) because I used to sing this to him when he was a baby,

"Do you remember, the twenty-eighth day of September."

Now Maurice White (lead singer of The Elements as they are affectionately known) sings the twenty-first day of September (incidentally my beloved aunt Debbie's B-Day), but I changed it to suit this awesome newborn son of mine!

Of course, this was such a joyous occasion, but so too, was our first anniversary and I was intent on getting at least a card for my husband, the new daddy! My mother had come to help with the baby and drove me to the grocery store. It must've taken me thirty minutes to get that card, but I did it. You should know that I had to have an episiotomy with Christopher. No woman ever wants to be cut "down there" (and it's not where you *think* it is). When the hospital level drugs wore off, let me tell you, the pain was almost unbearable. It made simply sitting in a chair difficult, going to the bathroom was torture, and walking was quite slow going, but I was going to deliver for my guy on our first anniversary.

Being a newlywed can be great, and then you throw a baby in at the beginning of a marriage, I do believe it took a toll as all of our attention and focus was on not breaking this gift from God. I panicked about everything! I was in labor a long while with Chris. He was in the birth canal for a long time before coming out (the kid had a big head and he was face down instead of up, making it more difficult to push him out), so when he finally came out, his head looked like a straight-up football! And his feet were both completely inverted towards each other. "Oh Lord," I thought, "he's gonna have to wear special shoes! I had to wear braces on my legs at night when I was a little kid. He's already going to have a hard-enough time being a Black man in America. *Now* he is going to have to wear special shoes and his head will be misshapen!" The pediatrician on call and our regular pediatrician both promised that both would be fine, but I recall telling Ed that, "they do not know what they are talking about," and that we needed to prepare for our son to be relentlessly teased. Silly new Mom! Of course, both resolved very quickly (though that kid does still have a big head, that's genetic), and just like that, we passed our first parenting challenge.

I only took six-weeks off from work and quickly returned to my job as a Commercial Flooring representative driving all over the tri-state area. Sure, I would've enjoyed more time off, but I was still a short-tenured employee and six weeks with full pay was the maximum I could take, plus, we were young (ahem, and still somewhat broke) so back to work I went.

Ed's job was going well at the time, but I do recall feeling that one female co-worker, while friendly with me, was a little *too* friendly with him. I did say something about my feelings and he dismissed me as maybe being a bit paranoid. It took him a while to start trusting my female intuition. Even when I couldn't put my finger on something specific, I was usually on to something. Maybe this is because he enjoyed the attention.

One of the things we've heard our previous church Pastors say is that if you are not giving your spouse the attention they desire, telling them they look good before they walk out of the house every day, that you appreciate the big and the little things they do to support the union, someone else will. Well, another lowercase "v" vow I had made internally, was that I was not prepared to stroke *any* man's ego. I mean, after all, growing up, my Mom would always tell me that I was the prize! If a man didn't act right, that they were just like buses and another would be along in ten minutes. While this advice isn't necessarily bad, especially when you are young and do not want to base your self-esteem on what a guy thinks of you, a lesson that I have learned, is that ALL men have egos, even mine and if I wasn't feeding it, another woman would. That said, it is important to acknowledge that the same is true for women. Fellas, if you don't tell her she's beautiful, has a nice butt (sorry to be so blunt, but every girl wants to hear it), and that you deeply desire her, there is always some dude wanting to do it for her.

It wouldn't be until 2013 during a couple's conference at our church, One Community, that I would learn that this emotional connection with another person happens well before anything physical and it is one of the nine steps in the path to an Affair (credit to Pastor Eric Wooten, who was our teaching Pastor at OneCC at the time).

The steps Eric lays out are:

1) Something causes you to lean away from your marriage (you are always either leaning in or out).
2) You become aware of another person and begin having lingering thoughts about them.
3) Innocent meetings between the two of you, open the door to flirting with the other person. NOTE: this is the step that alarm bells should be going off and is the last,

easiest place to step right on off this path, lest you continue down the slippery slope.

4) Meetings become intentional and planned by one of the people involved.

5) The two of you linger and hang out longer together even in a group setting.

6) You start talking about your feelings. These aren't feelings about each other necessarily, but feelings about things in general. Feelings are a level of intimacy that should only exist with your spouse - so this is far more dangerous than it may sound.

7) Isolated meetings between just the two of you, under the disguise of a legit purpose.

8) The two of you meet strictly for pleasure. At this point, you are running *straight* into destruction and you do not care; as the young people say, you are willing to risk it all.

9) Physical interaction becomes intimate and passionate

If you are married, happily or otherwise, we **highly** suggest you view the condensed version of that sermon we heard, on Eric's YouTube channel Relationshots. It is critical to watch this BEFORE you need it, trust me on this!

He-Do:

SUMMERTIME (DJ JAZZY JEFF AND THE FRESH PRINCE)

After the decision to move to Philadelphia and informing both families that we were moving in with each other, we still had to work on timing, and more importantly, I needed a J-O-

B. Looking back at all of this, I knew I was out of my element because I was a planner who liked to think about all angles and figure things out. I love to question and come up with scenarios for success and determine alternatives in the event of failure. I'm sure this gave Stacia angst because as good as a planner she is, she also doesn't like to overthink and leans toward actions instead. We would both struggle early on in our relationship with this dichotomy as we often wanted to get to the same conclusion on any particular decision, but we had different journeys in arriving to them.

Moving had also caused me some unease because I had to figure out what to do with all my "single guy" furniture and determine what stuff we were still going to need. To me, it seemed to be moving very fast and I was out of my element of control, where I felt like I had been able to know what and how I was going to manage and handle things. Now I have gained more responsibility for more than just myself and I had to learn on the fly to balance the urge to make decisions based solely on my assessment, and instead, that I needed to include Stacia on everything from major purchases, selection of utilities, and how money was going to be managed.

The other challenge I had to face with the move to Philadelphia was that my mom had moved in with me after she moved back to Michigan. I was letting her stay with me temporarily until she got on her feet, but because of her mental illness and the need for her to get professional help, my good deed was turning into a nightmare. One of my aunts tried to warn me that trying to support my mom was a huge responsibility and that I would struggle. I was unaware of just how bad my mom's condition could be especially when she was not taking her medication. The situation took a turn for the worse when about two to three months before moving to

Philly, my mom started on a downward mental spiral that I thought was going to surely give Stacia pause. Would she be able to handle our relationship knowing this was part of my reality?

When I told my mom that Stacia and I were very serious about our relationship and that I was moving to Philadelphia with her, she was not prepared to have me move–and especially not ready for the thought that our relationship had just kicked into a higher gear. She took the news harder than I thought and then filed a tenant-landlord injunction against me. This meant that I could not remove her from my apartment as now she had established residency in MY place! Even with the mental illness, I learned my mom could be quite crafty when it came to her survival. I was forced to pack up my belongings, end my lease, and provide her 30-day-notice that I was giving up my apartment and moving to Pennsylvania. On my last day in Michigan, I drove her to a homeless shelter and I had to tell her there was no way I could manage to support her and that I had to live my life. I felt like crap. I cried as she got out of the car and said to me, "Well, I hope this was worth it. I will probably be dead in a few weeks, so you won't have to worry about me anymore." Two months later, I found out that she had secured her own place and was able to get some financial assistance, along with a psychiatrist to counsel her. I told you, my mom was resourceful and creative when she had to be.

All of my worrying about this move was for naught, as God had already predetermined so much for us and ordered our steps. Much of what needed to happen fell into place quickly and neatly so we never had a chance to stress. I obtained a job via the old method of cold calling companies and recruiters and using my work fax machine to send out my resume. Stacia's job took care of nearly all of our moving expenses including temporary housing. I was able to sell off a majority of my belongings that were not needed in the new apartment and secured a moving van to take my stuff from East Lansing to King of Prussia, PA. I was even able to convince my best friend to come with me and we pulled a 48-hour weekend of driving, unloading the truck, and getting back to Michigan for him to make it to his job at the start of the week! Even today he and I talk about how crazy that was, and how fortunate we were to not have crashed the moving truck since we were running on fumes.

Once we settled into our new life as Pennsylvanians and squared away the apartment situation, we began to live our lives as a couple in earnest. We settled into our new routines and began to strengthen our bond. We navigated joining our finances together and developed a spending and savings plan. We both agreed it was important to get connected to a local church and began to look around at our options. Our backgrounds in religion were quite different as I had spent most of my teenage years being part of a Missionary Baptist Church while Stacia had grown up in the African Methodist Episcopal (AME) church. Initially, I was not a fan of being part of the AME church as I saw it as old, stuffy, and too complicated with its rules and procedures surrounding its liturgy. However, Stacia had never known anything else and was adamant that I at least give it a try. I knew it was the right thing to do, and I was willing to be open to it because we agreed that having a faith-based relationship along with a connection to a church would strengthen us and our relationship with God.

We settled on joining Mount Zion AME church in Devon, PA, after visiting several churches in the area. I don't think either of us knew how impactful this little church would be in our relationship and our lives. It was from this little church we would gain a deep connection to not only the community but to several individuals who would become our extended family while we lived in the Philadelphia area. When you join a new church, especially a small one, you hope to feel welcome and we found just that. We were welcomed with open arms. Not only because we were taking this important step in our faith, but we were newbies (i.e. fresh blood) of which the church was in dire need. It wasn't long before both Stacia and I found ourselves on every committee and church group at Mt. Zion. We both even found ourselves in the choir! For those who know me and are reading this, you must be shaking your head. "Ed? In the choir?" Yes, I was. Tone-deaf and all, up there singing the praises to our Heavenly Father. Shaking my head now, I will admit I was awful! Stacia tried to help me, but I can't sing a lick and it was easy to tell I was not born with the gift of song. I was looking like the "black" Forrest Gump in the choir stand trying to catch the beat. Every once in a while, I would stay in pitch, which was a surprise even to our choir director.

Within a few months into living in Philly (really King of Prussia), it became apparent that this arrangement of shacking up needed to be a short-term living situation. In other words, Stacia was like, "Hey, you know we are not going to be living like this forever, right?" So, the time came for us to choose a ring, determine when we were going to get engaged, and more importantly, the timing for our nuptials. There is nothing like a woman on a mission with the goal in sight of tying the knot. It wasn't like I didn't want to get married, but I was definitely in the mindset of "why rock the boat when we are doing just fine?" In my mind, the plan should have been to live together for about two to three years, save up enough money for a down payment for a home, and then set a date within a three to a five-year window, once we were financially secure. As you can tell, and if you've been reading closely, this was a flawed train of thought on my part that was going to get me kicked out of the apartment and lose my girlfriend! I do remember several intense conversations around where the relationship was heading and that she wasn't heading into her 30's trying to have babies. Given our financial situation and the need to show this woman she was the most important thing to me, I bucked up and built an elaborate plan to first get a ring and propose to her before I lost everything.

One of the good things about living in the Philly area was the access we had to Jeweler's Row, which is one the largest and oldest diamond district in America, second only to the one in New York City. With an idea of the cost and a credit card in my shaky hand, we took to the streets of Jeweler's Row to find the perfect ring. I will give Stacia credit as she is a very conscientious spender and will search for the most ideal option before dropping any large amounts of money on a purchase. The ring she liked the most was very nice, and it wasn't going to break the bank. The next important step was finding the right opportunity to propose, all while not showing my hand, so that this could be one of the most romantic experiences of Stacia's life.

I like to think of myself as a romantic who has a knack for planning a grand and special event when it comes to the woman of my life. Up until this point, most of my romantic escapades with Stacia centered around cards, handwritten poetry, and the occasional dozen roses. For this proposal, I needed to take it to the next level. In the late fall leading up to December of '95, I surveyed several co-workers from the area and was recommended a quaint French restaurant that was perfect. I won't re-tell the whole story of getting her to this place and the drama that ensued in trying to keep this a surprise since she has already laid that out, but suffice it to say, a brother was nervous. Getting to this point in my life was a major step in finally having something I had been searching for my entire life, a soul mate. There were only a few times in my life where I felt even remotely this close to someone, but Stacia was the only one whom I saw myself with forever. As with most men, I wanted to be a good provider, a better mate, and ultimately share in the experience of raising kids.

There were some twists and turns along the way to our nuptials, and many things that came up eventually were set aside as the focal point became getting to the altar. Like most couples, we argued and fought over silly things that we would both say were minor. Those minor things grew into problems for us later down the line because we weren't doing the work to uncover the deeper underlying issues at hand. I was the type of person who saw nothing wrong with still being friendly with ex-girlfriends and I never discussed with Stacia the impact that this had on her and how it made her feel. It would be years before I would finally take off my blinders and be open to conversations that would make me feel uncomfortable. I struggled early on with being able to be still in the moment and hear a different perspective on a situation that I was ready to dismiss.

We plowed on through the months leading up to the wedding, and lucky for us, our love for each other carried us through. Both sides of the family were supportive and actively participated in the planning, with Stacia's side financially supporting a majority of the costs. We were able to include a lot of friends, family, and even Mt. Zion members in our ceremony which made for a special day. The most memorable parts of the wedding were having two preachers managing the nuptials, our Mt. Zion choir who came from Pennsylvania, and Stacia's former hairdresser who sang two songs in a sequined vest all while using a microphone connected to a portable speaker. I was even able to use my old supervisor from MSU as our cameraman, for only the cost of a bottle of liquor! Let's just say that you get what you pay for.

Following our whirlwind engagement and marriage, we were married and officially Mr. and Mrs. Edward Gowens. Following our honeymoon in the Poconos, it was time for the next phase of life, planning a family and moving from an apartment into a home. Realizing that we needed extra loot to accomplish this, I moonlighted as a telemarketer selling credit cards. It was a tough nine-months, even though I excelled at this job, I knew that long term I was not interested in having to do this again. I felt a lot of pressure to not let Stacia down as well as to figure out if my career was on the right track.

Before we knew it, we were pregnant with our first child and it felt as though life kicked into a whole different gear. Now I was not only responsible for the two of us, but now the new addition to our family. My head was spinning with how much life with a kid was going to cost, were we moving too fast, and was I capable of helping to raise a child. I was having serious jitters and feeling a little lost. But in typical Stacia fashion, she was all in and she had enough confidence for both of us. It was her focus and determination that pulled me to keep up and not linger too long in my fear of messing this all up. And one of the happiest moments of our lives happened when our son was born, on September 28, 1997.

We had settled into a condo in a suburb called Limerick and began life as suburbanites who were married with children. Shortly after Christopher's birth, Stacia decided she wanted to go back to school to get her MBA and enrolled as a part-time student. We managed as best we could, but this was a lot of stress on a young marriage. A newborn, finances are still funny, and now more responsibility was falling on me to manage the household while she attended classes. At this point, doubt began to creep into my mind, and I started to feel as though so much of what we were doing was more about achieving Stacia's goals and I was being pulled along for the ride. Like so many men, I kept it to myself and we seemed to only discuss it as it crept into conversations as side snide remarks to each other about what one of us was *or* was not doing.

Adding insult to injury, it seems the next thing I knew, the plan was changing again and now we were heading back to Michigan for her to continue her MBA at MSU as a full-time student. We tussled back and forth about this decision because I didn't understand how this was going to all work out and wasn't she already in an MBA program? I soon learned that when God has a plan for you, he has your back, no matter how impossible the situation seems He will work it out. Taking difficult situations into your own hands is not a good idea.

We-Do:
NOW THAT WE FOUND LOVE (HEAVY D & THE BOYZ)

During this time, we did grow a lot together. We learned how we could agree on what an end goal was, i.e. let's have a baby, yet respect each other's differing paths or timelines in achieving those goals. Or at least, that's what we thought we were doing! Stacia readily admits she was BORN without patience and oftentimes Ed is more methodical, he looks at every issue 40 different ways which could be exhausting to her. We had achieved a lot during our short three-year relationship; we had moved halfway across the country, started new jobs, gotten engaged, bought our first home, gotten married and had a child. All of this, mind you, living far away from family and long-time friends so all we had was each other. We think that this did provide us with a CMB (Cash Money Brothers - the criminal syndicate in the movie New Jack City) mentality, "We all we got!" We didn't make any significant decisions without truly engaging each other. We developed a respect for the other person's way of thinking and navigating life. We eventually learned how to make compromises, though Ed probably felt that he was the one compromising the majority of the time. This is not to say there were not issues that continued to be swept under the rug. Stacia has already outlined for you that she was less than trusting of women from Ed's past. We never really discussed these things and we should have. Stacia would just get upset with Ed for not understanding her perspective. Ed thought it was no big deal that Stacia was overreacting and didn't proactively address her concerns. So now, we had this new love, new marriage, new child...what were we going to do with it?

Mentors! If you don't have one, GET ONE!

(Nod to one of our favorite movies - Toy Story). Looking back, one thing we did not have during this extremely hectic time in our marriage, that we clearly needed were mentors. Marriage mentors. People who we could talk with independently and/or as a couple who could not just give us advice on how to handle any one situation, but who could hold us accountable to how we ought to treat one another. How Ed should *love* Stacia (like Christ loved the church right? He *died* for his bride, so that's *a lot* of love). That Ephesians 5:25-29 kind of love—unconditional—even if he didn't feel like it. Meaning, no matter if he got something in return. And how Stacia should *respect* Ed. Now some of the fellas are, no doubt, saying to themselves, "I gotta *die*, but she just has to respect me? That hardly seems like a fair deal!"

The definition of respect according to dictionary.com is *a feeling of deep admiration for someone or something elicited by their abilities, qualities, or achievements*. If we stop to think about it, respect is very much connected to a word we've already mentioned, that has a negative connotation: ego.

Understand (don't fight) God's design!

A man needs to know his woman deeply admires his abilities. To hear with regularity that she appreciates his kindness, the fact that he does the dishes, that he cooks dinner and changes diapers just like she does, that he earns money to keep their family safe and protected. In short, she needs to feed that ego and for an independent, smart, accomplished woman, this was a big struggle for Stacia. Oh, she told her girlfriends all about how wonderful he was, but that message didn't seem to land on the one who needed to hear it most, Ed. Likewise, Ed needed to communicate through both deeds and words how much he loved his wife and relished in his role as her #1 champion. That she was more beautiful than the day before and he would spend his life demonstrating he was up to the task of loving her being measure.

We wished that we understood that God designed husbands to love and wives to respect and every time we decided not to walk in concert with that design, we were hurting our relationship, each other, and our Heavenly Father.

CHAPTER 4

She-Do:

YOUR LOVE KEEPS LIFTING ME HIGHER (JACKIE WILSON)

Truthfully, with Ed by my side and all that we had done within our short relationship, moving in together, getting married, buying a house, having a kid, I felt unstoppable. That's why I felt so comfortable in deciding to leave my job and my part-time MBA program (which said the job was paying for) to move back to Michigan to go to business school full time. I had a big dream, working for a pharmaceutical company in marketing and ascending that corporate ladder. It was a struggle for him, as you've read, but he agreed, and we packed up our first home and moved back to Michigan and into my Mother's house. The adjustment was a tad rough, it's hard being a grown-up kid with a kid living in your Mom's house. Roles seemed to get confused – and we had our fair share of, "yes, I am YOUR child, but this is MY child, I got this," moments.

We moved back to Michigan in September of 1998 as I had been accepted in the Eli Broad Graduate School of Management's (MSU) accelerated MBA program and even obtained a graduate assistantship to help offset tuition.

Side note: The Assistant Dean of Multicultural Affairs at the College of Business was a mentor of mine, a friend of the family, and he helped me secure my place in the program. It is so important to build relationships with people, live up to your end of the deal (maintaining the appropriate GPA, which I have to admit, classes like Statistics didn't make a foregone conclusion, achieve a decent score on the GMAT, etc.).

The coursework was to begin in January 1999 with classes through the Summer and graduation only eighteen months later in May 2000 (two thousand zero-zero party over, oops, out of time). Because we were down to one income, we couldn't afford to do a big celebration for our third wedding anniversary, so we got a room at the Comfort Inn in Okemos, MI. My people from Lansing will remember this was the hotel that had hot tubs in the room—aye! Well, we had BIG fun (like Vanessa did in that one episode of the Cosby show). So big that in October, we learned that we would be welcoming baby number two. SURPRISE!

I panicked at first. "We have one income, my husband drives an hour and a half each direction in earning this one income, I will be in class, working or studying until late into the evening every day, and we will have two mouths to feed," I said to myself. "I can't do this." When I told my Mom of our coming attraction, she looked at me and said, "You're not fifty. You'll figure it out!"

And with that, I had to buck up and motor on (see what I did there a nod to Motor City).

Thankfully my morning, or should I say, all day sickness with this pregnancy lasted only a couple of weeks and Christopher could be easily placated with a constant rerun of his favorite Barney and friends VHS tape. When it was time for me to start classes in January, I was feeling good. I recall my first conversation with my first-year cohort, the group we were attached to for all of our classes/projects for the entire first year of the program. I started, "Well, I know I just met you all, but I should tell you that, I found out I'm pregnant and the baby is due in late June. Smack dab in the middle of our Summer classes. I obviously can't pinpoint the date and promise that it won't be on the day we have some capstone presentation, but I can promise you that I will work my hardest all the way up to the day I need to deliver the baby and I will come back as soon as possible." Their jaws dropped, but what choice did they have but take me at my word?

Can you picture this? Me wobbling to and from class, my work as a graduate assistant, study groups, and exam cramming sessions. I got in front of my classmates from all over the world with my big ole pregnant belly for presentations, and I excelled in my courses! One of my classmates was constantly worried that my water would break in class and that they would have to get me to the hospital because Ed worked so far away. I appreciate how quickly bonds formed in my MBA class and I appreciate knowing I had back up if Ed wasn't immediately available.

On the night of June 22, 1999, the night before I had a scheduled appointment with my OB-GYN, I knew something wasn't right. Super painful contractions that would come in five minutes, then eight minutes, then two-minute increments, and then stop altogether for two hours. I asked Ed to stay home and go with me to the doctor just in case. Mom had an interview for the principalship at the high school she graduated from in Grand Rapids, MI, and instructed me to "Not have the baby until I get back!" I made no promises!

When I showed up at the doctor's office, she told me to lay back for my measurements and exclaimed, "Girl, you are four centimeters dilated. Get over to the hospital right now!" I don't always follow directions, but this one I certainly did. I didn't, however, follow Mom's direction of waiting until she got back and her namesake, our baby girl Alexa Diane Gowens, was born at 2:25 pm on June 23, 1999. We were over the moon! We got a perfect little girl, even though she didn't like me at all for the first six months of her life because I was never home. I returned to school two weeks after giving birth via Cesarean section, ready to kick butt and take names. My team was nice enough to record Finance classes for me and then brought them to my house before returning to classes, so I could watch them while nursing the baby. So much fun for a marketing major, but I made it through. I took the Finance final as soon as I returned to campus and got a 3.5 in the class. Listen, that had to be God because our professor was notorious for creating exams that didn't contain anything taught in his lectures or from our book.

This was a time in my life that I wholeheartedly believed that dreams do come true! With a lot of help from family and friends and Ed's unyielding support, I successfully graduated with my MBA with a concentration in Marketing in May of 2000. I also secured my dream job of marketing for Eli Lilly and Company in Indianapolis, IN.

Ed was quickly swooped up by Lilly as well. They wanted him to start before I had even finished school, but still offered him a job beginning in June which is when my new adventure was set to begin.

While Lilly employees, we built a strong network, lifelong friendships, and church homes in Indianapolis and Sterling Virginia, where we moved when I was promoted to District Sales Manager and Ed continued working in IT at a planned new manufacturing site. The kids adjusted well with the moves to and from Virginia and soon, we were back in Indianapolis when I got the opportunity to return to my previous workgroup.

These six years, moving to Indianapolis, to Virginia, and back again with increasing job responsibility seemed to go smoothly, at least from my perspective. Not so for Ed. Because he is not a "rock the boat" kind of guy, he silently resented the fact that I didn't say "thank you" or recognize how hard he worked to keep the whole G-Team machine moving. In my mind, it was clear I was grateful for the fact that he cooked, cleaned, did laundry, and was an attentive and involved parent. I mean, I did all of these things too. I just felt like everyone was working hard and there was no need for a "thanks" to either one of us for doing what was required to maintain a family. We never talked about his feelings about this, and that was a problem. A big one.

Fast forward to Spring 2009. We had recently experienced the pure, unadulterated joy and pride of traveling as a family to Washington DC for the inauguration of Barack Obama. Ed and I took a short trip to Cleveland to see the Alvin Ailey dancers, who I love, and spent a quiet romantic weekend in April. By mid-May, my entire world fell apart.

I was downstairs and hopped on the computer, probably to check Facebook, and noticed that Ed had left his email open. There, I read a lengthy email exchange between Ed and a woman that he worked with who lived in New Jersey. There before my eyes were all of the sweet nothings. All of the reminiscences of their weekend together during his recent business trip. The songs that reminded him of her. The explicit details. I immediately felt sick to my stomach.

While I honestly believe I have blocked out many of the details of that day, I remember emailing this woman a very nasty note warning her that regardless of what happened with us, she was being canceled immediately! He was upstairs, and the kids were outside in the neighborhood playing, *thank God*. We had a huge framed picture of us that had once sat outside of our wedding reception and was now mounted on the wall in our bedroom. I stormed up the stairs, snatched it off of the wall, and screamed a blood-curdling scream while slamming it to the ground. We were broken, so the picture of us looking blissfully happy should be too. He ran in the room, "What's going on?"

I called our friends, The Pletchers, who lived on the west side of the city and through uncontrollable sobbing, managed to ask if the kids could spend the night, and please, do not ask any questions and they did so without hesitation. We will circle back to how important it is to have your village built and solid *before* you need it!

Before cleaning my face up so I wouldn't look crazy as I left the house to find the kids, I told Ed that I knew what had happened and that we would be talking about it when I got back. This is when a mother's protective instinct kicked in big time. I couldn't let my children know what I had learned. *Your dad is a lying, cheating, asshole,* is what I wanted to say, but I calmly collected them around the corner and spun a story about how their "play" aunt and uncle wanted them to come to spend the night.

Side note: They had a ball that night too. The Pletchers were always big fun and I am so grateful that they made sure my kids enjoyed themselves, not knowing what they may return home to.

There was a lot of screaming and crying and pleading for forgiveness. But I had made a Capital "V" vow to myself, remember? I would never stay with someone who cheated on me. I'd seen it before and I would *not* let myself become one of those 'weak' women who stayed in a relationship after infidelity. I mean, once a cheater, always a cheater, right? I learned how long the affair had gone on and, as is customary, it started as an emotional connection. He would share how he cleaned the house, picked up the dry cleaning, and picked up the kids from school and she lavished him with praise. "You are such a good man. If you were mine…." He felt validated and decided to make their relationship physical one weekend.

I was absolutely devastated and wanted to fight. I wanted to run. I wanted to curl up in a ball and die. I emailed her from his email address, called her everything but a child of God, and let her know that her little affair was over-over and that she had better watch her back because it was not above me to ride out to New Jersey with my crew. The fact that she emailed back a very nasty message about things she'd done with my husband added fuel to my already raging fire and I immediately made him change his cell phone number and his email address. A couple of days later, I was contacted on Facebook by *her* husband. That's right, she too was married!

He shared with me that he knew about the affair and had gone to the hotel where the two of them hooked up. He was on the verge of going in, finding their room, and wrecking shop, but the thought of what would happen to their young son if he went to jail weighed heavily enough for him to get in his car and go home. My heart broke again, *for him*. A man I had never met. I could just imagine how awful a decision it was to have to make and that it was my husband that caused him such grief. We stayed in touch for a while early on in the revelation of our spouses' infidelity. Strangely, I suppose it felt like no one else in the world could possibly understand the pain we were going through. Through our conversations, I learned that before Ed and his wife had become intimate, he had called my house and spoken to Ed, warning him to stay away from his wife.

So, in addition to being careless and thoughtless about our relationship, I felt that Ed was careless about his safety and our children's. He had put us all in jeopardy with his continuous pursuit of this female (yep, still bitter y'all, but please give me grace, God is still working on me). The truth of the matter is, he didn't really know her, and the crazy stories highlighted on shows like Snapped or anything on the ID channel are fraught with a woman who feels jilted or wants to take the wife's place and the worst happens. He didn't know her husband, maybe he was a guy with nothing to lose and was willing to take anyone out who threatened the sanctity of his home. I was *beyond* furious with him putting me, the kids, and even himself in potential harm's way.

As we fought that night, really, I guess it was me fighting and him apologizing, I honestly believed it would be the last we ever slept under the same roof (remember the Vow) and my head was spinning. After more than ten years, this is how our relationship was going to end. In the image of that shattered picture frame on the floor of our bedroom.

I didn't want to eat and would cry for hours just looking out the window. At the time, Chris Brown's song *Damage*, was on repeat in my car to and from work:

> *"Look at the damage (the damage)*

The damage

Damage that I've caused you (that I've caused you)

I know I broke your heart

Cause I did you wrong

Now look at the damage

Look at the damage that I've caused

The dumbest decision that I made that I ain't proud of

A few hours that meant absolutely nothing cost me your love..."

I often wondered to myself if Ed felt that way about the damage he'd done.

He-Do:

WHEN A MAN LOVES A WOMAN (PERCY SLEDGE)

As life progressed for us, we fell into our routines as most married couples do. When we decided to move back to Michigan, we were only a few years into our marriage so there was still plenty we were getting used to. With a baby in the mix, it added many beautiful firsts for us in addition to struggles, and challenges that befall young couples. As you read earlier, I am a planner and a thinker who always liked to have option one, and option number two, with at least two to three backup plans on top of that. One of my challenges was just being there for Stacia without making it sound as though I was belittling her plans or thoughts. She would want to talk through our plans and situations, but I preferred to talk a little, make the decision by having many internal conversations with myself and then execute. I certainly didn't like to revisit discussions over and over again.

When she presented her plan to move from Pennsylvania back to Michigan to attend MSU for her MBA instead of the local Penn State campus, I was confused. I thought to myself, "She's already in an MBA program. Plus, how are we going to pay for this? And why now? Where were we going to live? What were we going to do with our townhouse that we just purchased in Limerick?" When I expressed my concerns and questions to her during the early stages of planning you would have thought I had taken her to Judy Judge and hired Johnny Cochran to represent me! Now, of course, I'm over exaggerating but this is what it felt like as we debated back and forth. Looking back at this major milestone, I believe I had not yet fully understood that I was married to a person who was always looking to better herself and was always ready for a challenge. She saw her career was limited in its current state, and if she ever wanted to achieve more, she needed to get more aggressive about her plans. Me dragging my feet would do little to assure her that I was going to be supportive and that I understood her perspective.

Eventually, I agreed with her, and the plan and accepted that this was going to be a positive move. Together, we were going to make it through this. Once we had the plan laid out, everything moved ahead at warp speed. Stacia was able to secure some funding for school so that we would be able to take out just a small loan to keep us afloat. We decided to keep the townhouse and rent it out, so we could at least cover the rent and continue homeownership. I was quickly able to secure a position as a contractor with GM in their IT department in their Truck Product Center, in Pontiac, MI. It was going to be a long haul from Lansing to Pontiac (60 miles one way), but it was the best salary that would provide us more income since I was going to have to be the single source of income for the next 18 months while she was getting her MBA.

As the plan came together and we were winding down our time in Pennsylvania, our last activity was to sell all of the unnecessary furniture we were not going to take with us. We advertised a yard sale and extended it to several friends to help move what was left. One of my female friends that I had worked with came over and purchased a few items. Stacia mentioned this earlier in her chapter regarding her "sixth sense" about this former co-worker, and how I was oblivious to potential overtures by other women. What I interpreted as just a friend coming to help us out turned into a discussion about looking at the signs, and how I had missed all of them. This woman came by, stayed, and talked to both of us, but when I walked her out to their car with what she had purchased, we talked for another 30 minutes. Stacia was wondering, why did it take so long to say goodbye and get back to completing the move? What was so important that the conversation lingered so long? And more importantly, why couldn't I see it? I tried to assure her that it was nothing and that what she perceived was misguided and unfounded. It became a heated conversation about me and how I was not supporting her in this move, and more importantly, not believing her assessment of the situation and how easily I was dismissing it. In typical guy fashion, I was lost, confused, and frustrated! How did I all of a sudden become the "villain" in this situation when I had not done anything? In my mind, I was just talking with a friend about our new adventure and a bunch of other chit-chat that was completely innocent in nature.

I would learn later through counseling and revelation from sermons from our different pastors over time, that, at times when conflict did arise between us, the time to work through the situation was right when it happened and that we should talk, in detail, about each other's feelings. Instead, I would become defensive, shut down, and ignore her feelings, but in a nice way. This passive-aggressive pattern of behavior proved to be disastrous and had a long-term impact on our relationship. I had become the king of the "No comeback", as I rarely ever wanted to rehash our issues, especially if it involved something she'd felt I'd done (though I didn't have an issue coming back at her with the… OK, OK, but what about when you…")

My M.O. was to chalk it up to her being "emotional" and that she was looking for ways to control my feelings and my interactions with other people, especially women. I was digging myself into a hole in more ways than one, and I was going to end up paying the ultimate price for my inability to communicate with Stacia.

We moved back to Michigan in 1998 and were able to plan with Stacia's mother to live with her during Stacia's 18-month MBA program at MSU. This was not an easy decision to make, as I did not want to be a burden on her family. But I also realized that we were not financially stable enough to have a mortgage in Limerick to manage, along with paying separate rent in Lansing. I was also slightly traumatized from my experience of how Stacia, her mom, and her sister were at odds early on during our dating. Flashback: Stacia's sister was a teenager and my mother-in-law was an assistant principal, with Stacia having taken up residency in the basement during her last year of college. Early on in our dating I would come over and spend the night, only to be awakened every morning by yelling and door slamming because Stacia's mom was ready to go and her sister was literally running late every morning. It was so bad one time that one morning, Stacia angrily jumped out of bed, grumbled and stomped her way upstairs, and threatened them both! I thought to myself, "What in the Sam Hill have I gotten myself into?"

Once Stacia and I got settled, we started to enjoy the benefits of being so close to family and to many of our friends who were still local to either Lansing or Detroit. My mom was ecstatic to have us back in Michigan so that she could spend more time with her grandchildren. Stacia's aunt and uncle were close by in East Lansing, and her grandparents from Louisville were regularly on the road to visit everyone so it started to feel like this move benefited us in multiple ways. As the school year was about to begin for her program, I thought to do something special for our three-year anniversary by booking us a jacuzzi suite at the Comfort Inn. I spared no expense and went all-in with wine, fresh fruit, and massage oils. Needless to say, we had a good time. A really good time—and that is how baby number two was made! It came as a surprise to us, and really to me because I prided myself on my "pull out" game being tight! I guess God had to remind me that it really wasn't as good as I thought.

With baby number two on the way and Stacia's MBA course work kicking in, it added a new level of stress to our relationship. We would soon have two kids to support and care for, one parent going full-time in a condensed master's program, and one parent traveling 60 miles one way for work. After about six months of this, I felt like I was dying. It was bad enough with the commute but managing a newborn with a toddler became downright insane. We were both struggling to find time for our new family, let alone time for ourselves. We would pass each other in the hallway from either her going and coming from class, and me trying to juggle much of the household responsibilities.

I was trying to be a trooper, realizing that this was a short-term inconvenience with a big payout at the end once she completed her program. I thought to myself that this is love, and to be a good man, I needed to be there for her.

When a man loves a woman

Spend his very last dime

Trying to hold on to what he needs

He'd give up all his comforts

And sleep out in the rain

If she said that's the way

It ought to be...

The 18-months that Stacia spent in the MBA program seemed like a long dream, and there were plenty of sacrifices on both of our parts. Living at her mom's home was a blessing in disguise as it helped us keep our expenditures low, plus we did have the income from the townhome in Pennsylvania that was a bonus. However, not long after our tenants moved in we found out they were not as stable as we thought. We attempted to remain open and lenient, which made it even more frustrating as they were late almost every month with their rent payment. We eventually went through a painful eviction process and placed ourselves in a financial hole that would take us a while to crawl out from under.

On the surface, we were still functioning OK as a unit, as we were able to take care of our current financial responsibilities and we were closely monitoring our spending. However, I was increasingly feeling stressed as the wear and tear of driving a little more than two-hours a day for work and still having to take care of most home duties by myself. It tested my resolve. We tried to have some "us time", but with our schedules and the needs of the children, it was near impossible to do so consistently.

Side note: One of the best pieces of advice we got on raising children would come later when we lived in Virginia. Our Pastor told the congregation how important it was to truly love your spouse and not let the children become the sole focus of the relationship. We chuckle when we recall him saying, "those kids are going to leave you when they turn 18. The last thing you want is to look at your spouse in your empty nest and think, 'I don't even know you.'"

Carving out some "us time" was a missed opportunity for keeping our relationship refreshing and engaging. Low-level frustration grew within me. It was difficult sometimes to keep the big picture in mind in terms of the benefit to our whole family of Stacia having an advanced degree and the commensurate salary. At times, I could only see it from my perspective, what I was giving up in order to support her. As mentioned in earlier chapters, my ability to communicate and express this was non-existent, so the resentment was just fermenting. Because I feared how it would come across, and that it would portray me as being selfish and unsupportive, I was not willing to be open and honest. This bad habit of holding in my emotions was eventually going to be our downfall and lead us into the darkest chapter of our marriage.

Near the end of completion of the MBA program, Stacia had multiple offers to consider and we both let out a big sigh of relief as we could see the light at the end of the tunnel. She accepted a job in Indianapolis and I was also able to secure a job which meant a huge burden was going to be lifted off our shoulders. Now, if only we could get to Indianapolis in one piece. Here is why: right before we were to move, as in the night before, I had a going-away celebration at my job in Grand Rapids. Several of my colleagues were younger than me and they thought it would be fun to have drinks after work on my last day. *Bad idea. Horrible idea.* On that day, we left work early and headed to happy hour where I chilled for a few hours with the entire team. I had told Stacia I would probably be home around 8:00-ish. I don't remember how many shots of Tequila, whiskey, mixed drinks, etc. I had but let's just say, I left around 10:00 PM and had not made any effort to call Stacia.

To be fair, we did have cell phones as this was in the year 2000, and although we used them mostly for emergencies, I was typically good for calling home to let her know where I was or if I was running late. That night I did *not*. Instead, I made this about me and my need to hang out with my coworkers, living my best life, and drinking like I was 21. It wasn't until I was on my way home that I realized I had not called to check-in. As I was driving back to Lansing I realized I was in a dead zone with no signal. I knew I was going to get it! But there is more. Remember, I had been drinking, and drinking...and drinking. I now realized I was six sheets to the wind! There is no way I should be driving! My vision was blurry and I'm sure I was swerving, and the best thing I thought of was to pull over and get myself together. I found a spot off an exit ramp, rolled down my window, and tried to *will* myself to sobriety. This break turned into a 45-minute power nap! When I reached the house and walked in at a little past midnight (I think) I was greeted by an enraged wife who was losing her mind because she had no idea of where I was and if I was dead or not.

She laid into me something fierce and said that this was the stupidest "blankety-blank" I had ever done. I put my head down, mumbled I was sorry, and gave multiple excuses. If looks could kill, in the dark no less, the red in her eyes and the heat coming out of her mouth burned me to a crisp as if I had just been cremated. After basically no sleep, we woke up the next morning, headed to Indianapolis with this heavy burden and tension between us. It was a horrible drive as we discussed the previous evening and my escapades, and how I could put myself in that type of situation given where we were in our lives at that point. We were not kids, or youngsters, anymore. We were adults with a family and responsibilities and I no longer had the luxury to behave as some drunken fool.

I knew I had disappointed her. And she had every right to be upset. However, in my mind, this was just a "tiny" blip on the radar and was not representative of me as a whole. I think I may have even tried to defend myself with that perspective, which made the incident even worse. I still had not figured out how to communicate effectively, to engage her on what her feelings were and really listen to how my actions affected her. I believe that no matter my transgression, I would always present the fact that 9 out of 10 times I was making the right decisions, so a slip up here and there should not outweigh all of my good. In my head, this sounded simplistic and reasonable, but from my mouth to her ears it was a shock and an idiotic defense that showed I was not interested in her feelings, but my self-gratification. What I was failing to realize at this time was that while I was trying to keep score, I had done very little to build up any points in her emotional bank. I was trying to cash a check and there were insufficient funds in my "love account". Another lesson that I was not going to come to grips with until our counseling later on.

The move to Indianapolis turned into one of the highlights of our marriage. We were able to connect with new friends and reconnect with MSU alumni who I knew from my membership in NSBE (National Society of Black Engineers). We found a wonderful church home and a great community to raise our kids in as they each began to engage in various sports and extracurricular activities. On the work front, Stacia was quickly moving up the organization she was a part of, and I too was being recognized for completing key projects and deliverables that led to an acknowledgment from my management team. In short, life was on the upswing as we settled in "Naptown", and we adjusted nicely.

Just when I thought we were good with our lives and with what we had started, our time in Indy was short-lived when Stacia took a new opportunity within the company that moved us to the DC/Maryland/Northern Virginia area. For Stacia, this new chapter was her steppingstone into a management role and would be the needed experience for her career to continue to blossom. For me, it meant that I was going to have to "survive" and look to keep up with my superstar wife who I saw as a motivated machine. I knew this was all for the better, but I was feeling more as if I was being dragged along, and my career and my goals were taking a back seat to hers. The feeling of being an afterthought and having to make more sacrifices on my part was eating away at me. My ego and my need for affirmation were suffering, and yet I was not able to articulate this to my wife. In my mind, I convinced myself that she didn't care to know my feelings and it was better to keep them buried and work on pleasing her. By making her happy, I was sure to have her reciprocate that same love I thought I was giving to her. However, my thinking was flawed, and various chinks were already beginning to form in our marriage armor.

It was during this time that I secretly began to "experiment" with the internet and explored various pornography and dating sites. Initially, I was more voyeuristic and would read and view provocative profiles that interested me. There was no way I was going to slip up like other people do and get engaged in some type of online affair, I said to myself. First of all, I was too good for that, and besides, I was just reading and fantasizing. What harm was I actually doing? I would never commit the act of actually reaching out to someone and then hooking up. What fool would do that? You will see shortly, that I was *that* fool!

Let me state for the record that the internet is a wonderful tool that when used properly, and with the right intentions and proper boundaries in place, can provide unlimited possibilities, even in dating. With information at your fingertips, you can learn about any subject and can expand your intellect. All of this is available to you in the comfort of your home, or as we all now experience, in the palm of your hands via mobile devices. Just as wonderful as the internet can be, like with all man-made things, it is also a gateway into a pervasive world of lust, self-gratification, and infidelity. I can tell you first hand that once you start, no matter how innocently, using the internet (and now social media) as a means of escapism from your life, marriage, or work-life balance responsibilities, is a dead-end road.

Looking back at this crucial time in our marriage, it is apparent that I was a broken person. By broken, I mean I put myself into a position of thinking I alone could fix what was wrong in our marriage. I had closed off my true self to Stacia and was serving up lies to form her understanding of who her husband was. I was not being honest with myself and my issues, and I was in full denial of the impact my actions were causing to our marriage. I had begun to engage in destructive behavior to my marriage right under my wife's nose and was too self-absorbed to even consider her feelings. On the outside, many people viewed us as a "power" couple, with an awesome life and family. We were by all accounts, on the come up, and represented a pristine image of how love could and should look like. To make matters worse, I was getting so adept at living outside of myself, that even being as engaged in the church as we were, I had simply tuned out the correlations from weekly sermons that I know God was using to try and reach me. All of the warnings and lessons were right in front of me, giving me plenty of opportunities to turn away from my downward spiral, yet I ignored each one. My life and my marriage were teetering on the edge of a blade and it was only time before it was all going to come crashing down.

we-Do:
WHERE DO BROKEN HEARTS GO (WHITNEY HOUSTON)

There was a lot of yelling, screaming, and gnashing of teeth. There were children. Dear Lord, there were children we had to protect from all of this ugliness as we dealt with personal pain and interpersonal trauma. Shout out to our village, who without asking probing questions, we knew we could trust to "watch the kids for a little while" because it was going to be impossible to contain the rage and sadness as we bounced back and forth between the stages of grief like one of those rubber balls we used to use playing jacks (yeah, we're old). We wish we could say we had the presence of mind to know upfront what to do. How to take the first step. How to even exist in the same space.

Faith it 'til you make it.

In hindsight, one way we were able to do that was to continue in our faith. Ed did still have the gumption to actively suggest (sometimes every week), that we try and continue to go to church and that we begin attending couples counseling. Stacia was very hesitant but did end up complying with both. She remembers listening to Pastor Jeffrey A. Johnson (Eastern Star Church, Indianapolis) and being actively mad at God while he preached.

Pastor Johnson: "God so loved the world and he loves each and every one of his children."

Stacia: "You don't love me. If you did, you wouldn't have ripped my marriage apart."

Pastor Johnson: "God is a good God!"

Stacia: "Pastor says you're a good God. Humph well, not to me, how could you let this happen?"

There were many lessons learned through this painful experience and one was the truly unconditional love of God. Stacia in particular had a newfound understanding of what unconditional love meant. She was BIG MAD at capital H-I-M, yet God didn't banish her from His presence, cast her into the seventh circle of hell, or even suggest she wasn't allowed to feel the way that she did. Rather, He wasn't going anywhere, even if she didn't want Him around at the moment. She was His child and He was going to love her (and teach her) through the pain. When she reflects on this time, she can now smile and think to herself, "I was trying to get you to let me go, but you showed me the truth of Isaiah 41:13."

"For I, the Lord your God, hold your right hand; it is I who say to you, "Fear not, I am the one who helps you."

There were mornings she absolutely did not want to get out of bed. She did not want to go to work. It almost felt like she couldn't even breathe. And for quite some time, she certainly felt that her marriage to her best friend was over. But God helped her. To keep her in the palm of His hand. This time was also so difficult for Ed as he was left to wonder if she would ever forgive him, could he ever forgive himself? How did he let himself get to believing that having an emotional and physical relationship with another woman would make him feel better? Now he felt worse than he ever had - he had pierced the heart of the woman he truly loved. He put his family on the line.

If you see something, say something!

Ed knows that he should've spoken up. To say he wasn't feeling appreciated or respected instead of falling for the intoxicating fallacy of hearing that from complete strangers online and from another woman in bed. None of these women had to manage a day to day relationship with him, their children, her advancing education, her career. It was much easier to lavish praises from thousands of miles away. To live in a fantasy world with Ed's agent instead of the real, flawed man. If he'd spoke up, perhaps he wouldn't have walked every one of those steps in the path to an affair. A sin he certainly never set out to commit (this is where we point you back to Eric Wooten's YouTube channel *Relationshots* on the 9 Steps to an affair that was outlined in Chapter 3). The reality is no one wakes up one morning and says, "Today, I am going to cheat on my husband/wife," so it is essential to learn to spot the signs, while you have time to stop yourself from even taking Step One!

Bottom line: we both needed to be *much* better communicators. Ours was awful and that that was at the route of what led us down this current path. So many issues in a marriage can be tied to a breakdown in communication. For example, Ed didn't feel like Stacia valued him, until at one counseling session she told the therapist, "I had him on a pedestal, I thought he was damn near perfect." Ed's face was marked with surprise and said, "You did?" See, just because she didn't thank him for picking up the dry cleaning, she actually thought the world of him, but somehow, that wasn't computing to him. Oftentimes in a marriage, you can pass through each day with the quick, "Love you," on the way out of the door to work or before going to sleep. We've had to learn that having a dedicated time or cycle to go beyond the almost thoughtless, "Love you." We had talked past each other for so long and were fearful of having substantive and crucial conversations until Ed just stopped trying. Instead, he pointed his intention and affection to other women who offered the cheap, but quick thrill of feeding his ego. Stacia held her frustrations about their marriage in until Ed did something she didn't like and then exploded. It was impossible to tell at the time if we would ever survive Ed's ultimate betrayal and be able to salvage the marriage.

CHAPTER 5

He-Do:

CONFESSIONS (USHER) - ED'S STORY

Remember how earlier I arrogantly mentioned how I would never cross the line of doing more than just viewing illicit material on the internet? The fact that I was even in that position in the first place, should tell you all you need to know about how I was failing as a husband, as a person, and as a follower of Christ. I was addicted to the attention and the feeling that all of these inappropriate online interactions gave me. I continued to rationalize my secret life as a means of escapism that actually benefited me and allowed an outlet for my frustration. I was working hard to cover my tracks and to maintain the lie.

Emotionally I was detached from the marriage, but I was doing all of the operational duties that a husband should do. I kept up with my house chores, shuffled kids back and forth to school, kept up appearances in front of family and friends, and balanced my career. What I couldn't see, nor understand, was that I was so disconnected from my wife, that she was suffering alone in a marriage that was dying. My energy for her was way off and even though she couldn't put her finger on it at the time, I believe it's safe to assume that she felt deep inside something was off. When I was confronted by her about these feelings, I put on my dancing shoes and shuffled around key discussions like I was auditioning for a spot in the movie "A Chorus Line" (Note: This is one of Stacia's favorites).

After living in Northern Virginia for three years, we moved back to Indianapolis, and for a short time, I put more effort into focusing on us. Being back around friends and re-focusing myself on my career seemed to have a positive effect on me. But I slowly crept back into the bad behaviors. I was compartmentalizing my sin and unwilling to admit I was now on the path to destruction of my life as I knew it. I was conflicted with the guilt of what I was doing, while simultaneously maintaining a double life. This double life would come crashing down on me in a way I could never have ever imagined, and I was unprepared for.

Let's state it plainly and simply, I cheated. I had sex outside of our marriage. I lied about who I was talking to. I used emails and texts to carry out my unfaithfulness. I was no longer a faithful husband. I was no longer truthful. I was no longer the man she had fallen in love with. I rationalized my actions by thinking that I was getting something I needed, and I would know if I was really meant to stay in my marriage or not. The devastation I had caused was playing on the big screen right in front of my eyes, and I had a front-row seat. Even when confronted with some evidence of emails, call records, and inappropriate text messages, I continued to lie and hide behind misdirection and half-truths.

When you hide behind so many lies eventually all things come to light, and the impact on all people (children, family, friends, etc.) because of the illicit affair becomes a pain almost too great to bear.

I don't remember the specific day when I was finally caught. I can't tell you what time it was. What I can tell you is that I felt emotionally ill when I was confronted about the extramarital affair. I remember the pure horror of shock, confusion, and pain on Stacia's face. She went from emotionally devastated to enraged, and back again. There was yelling, cursing, and pushing. I could do or say nothing, just look dumbfounded. When I did finally try to speak between the yelling and cursing, what came out of mouth did nothing to infuriate her more. No amounts of "I'm Sorry" and "I don't know what I was thinking" was going to help the situation.

The pinnacle of this whole ordeal hit me like a brick as she was tearing through the house screaming, crying uncontrollably when she suddenly grabbed our portrait off the wall and slammed it to the ground with all her might. The entire frame, glass, and picture laid shattered on the floor. Just like that, I realized that this was symbolic in that I had shattered our marriage, and more importantly, I had shattered the image my wife had of me as a person and as her husband.

Reflecting back on what led me to initially cheat, I would say it came about due to my need to feel valued and appreciated. I was definitely feeling as though the marriage wasn't about me anymore, or about us, but more about my wife's feelings and what *I* was not doing to make *her* happy. I felt enormous pressure and that I alone, was responsible for making her happy and if she wasn't, it was because I didn't want to work at it. I couldn't (or maybe wouldn't) understand what was making her feel the way she was. Looking back at it now, I felt like most of our discussions pointed the finger at me about my shortcomings in the marriage, but never about what she wasn't doing. In some cases, her responses seemed to challenge the very reason we were even married, and I even began to question if this was all worth it. My response to these seemingly never-ending disagreements was shock after shock, overwhelming anger, and withdrawing from the relationship. In my mind, I was breaking my neck to help support the family, giving in to what she wanted, and I saw myself as sacrificing more than what she was giving me credit for. I could give her more if she would give me something in return, because wasn't marriage about balance? Were we not supposed to want to cater to one another?

I wasn't on a mission for a random hookup. What I wanted and felt I needed was a compassionate voice and interested party who was willing to side with me and confirm I was still a great guy and a great catch for anyone. I took and grew a friend-based platonic relationship with someone I knew casually. Connecting with someone else and feeding off the excitement of having someone feed into my ego, was what I felt I should have been getting at home. Having someone who agreed with me and comforted me, had a huge impact on my feelings and provided the excuse I needed to keep it going. Although the affair was providing a "happy place" for me to be myself (sort of), simultaneously there was also guilt.

During this affair, I wrestled with what I was doing and was ashamed. Deep down I wanted to be good, I did not want to be on this path and should have never put myself in this position. Oh God, what have I done? But true to form, during this darkest moment or our marriage, I took my little voice of reason and locked it away to minimize my guilt. I only cared about the here and now, and eventually I felt entitled to do what I was doing. I had to become cold and callous to dissociate from what I was doing.

As our marriage was disintegrating before my eyes, there was the realization that the impact of my actions wasn't just on me. I had now forced Stacia into action to protect the children as they were too young to handle the truths of a father who had betrayed their mother. She did, however, have me to talk to the children to explain that we were going to be handling things differently and that there would be changes to our living arrangement. I admitted to the children that I had hurt mommy's feelings and that I needed to do "some soul searching" which would require me to take some time for myself. I had not counted on managing the hurt and bewilderment that my children displayed while I danced around the fact that I had committed the ultimate sin. It was becoming apparent that in all my selfishness and self-gratifying actions, I had totally forgotten the key responsibility of being a father—which is to protect the family. I was now doing to my kids what I had promised myself I would never do, which was to leave them to grow up without a father just like I did.

Sitting here, stuck on stupid, trying to figure out

When, what, and how I'mma let this come out of my mouth

Said it ain't gon' be easy

But I need to stop thinking, contemplating

Be a man and get it over with, over with... [These are My Confessions]

I moved out to an extended stay motel near the house to give Stacia space as we tried to determine what our new normal was going to look like. The awful truth of what I did was drowning me and I finally reached out to a few of my closest friends to confide in them. It broke my heart to hear them respond that they had no clue I was going through so much and that I didn't think to talk with them. Each one of them was hurt and upset that I took matters into my own hands and that they would have never let me go down the path I chose. They felt as though if there was ever one couple that had it all together, it was the Gowens. As the questions mounted and even more confusion was expressed about how I let my marriage get to this point, I had to accept the fact that I tarnished my reputation and it would be an uphill battle to regain the respect of my friends. No one gave me any pity, although they each empathized with me on the difficulty of marriage. They reminded me that my wife was a gift from God and that the more responsible thing would have been to talk with her. If I didn't want to be married anymore I owed her the truth of coming clean. I needed to do some serious soul searching.

Another consequence of my betrayal was that not only did I impact my family, but the other person's family with whom I had the affair. Once the affair was revealed to both spouses, and when I learned that the husband of the woman I had an affair with had talked with Stacia and told her that not only had he previously called the house and told me to stop contacting his wife, but that he had actually come to the hotel where we spent the night together, I saw myself as a monster. I had turned into a neurotic and narcissistic man who allowed my issues of lack of communication and emotional intimacy to destroy the lives of multiple people. The gravity of the situation had reached critical mass and I needed to act. Either by working to save my marriage or taking the path to separation and divorce. Both paths weighed heavily on me, and I had no direction or vision.

Each day over the next few weeks was playing out like a horror movie as I began to accept the fact that I deserved to lose everything. I never imagined the growing feelings of betrayal not only to Stacia and the kids, to myself. Why couldn't I have avoided these set of circumstances that I placed everyone? One frightful conclusion I had to accept was that I had become so self-absorbed about what I thought I needed that even with my so-called common sense, I jeopardized everything about the life I had with my family and what God had been able to do for us. In addition, I felt like a total fool realizing that my selfishness and how I became tone-deaf to God's Word was the exact outcome that the devil wanted. I had fulfilled the enemy's goal of destroying God's love and image of marriage and was left with nothing but an empty hotel room with his sinister laugh playing in my head.

One evening while sitting alone in the motel, a voice suddenly spoke to me with a revelation. I was treating this situation as if I was alone. I was using my own limited mental and psychological experience to think through this damage which I would never be able to resolve on my own. Today, I believe that voice was God. In all of my self-absorption and self-gratification, I never fully turned to God for help and guidance. I had shunned the little voice in my head that was with me before I acted on my impulses and after. But now this voice was in stereo and it was in my head and in my heart. God had turned up the volume and I finally was in the right position to be receptive to what he had been broadcasting to me from day one. I was not alone, and that if I could re-commit to him and ask for the forgiveness of my sin, He could save my marriage. The voice made it clear to me it was only through Him that would I be able to change and reclaim what was lost. I cried and hung my head in shame because I was afraid that I had destroyed any chance of recovering my marriage. I remembered multiple conversations where Stacia said she would never accept being cheated on, and if it ever happened to us, she would be Audi-5000! But again, God's voice said that it was faith in Him alone that would save our marriage and that I would have to ask Jesus to bear this cross with me, as he did over 2,000 years ago when He died for my sins.

As we navigated our ugly new truth, life still had to go on. After a horrible winter following a family trip to California, I went to Stacia with the proposal of moving from the Midwest to a warmer part of the country. Initially she was hesitant and thought this would be too much for the kids. However, following that Snowmaggedon type winter we'd just endured, she agreed that relocating to warmer weather would be great. Initially, everything fell into place, from getting jobs to finding a home and getting the kids into school in our new hometown, in a suburb of Dallas. This had also provided Stacia and I a chance to reboot our relationship and for a minute it seemed like maybe the cloud we had been under for the past few years was finally lifting. But as they say, life has a funny way of throwing you a curve ball when you least expect it. During the couples retreat with our new church, Stacia pulled me aside to share with me something she could no longer hold in. It was now my turn to be on the receiving end of having been cheated on.

♪ CHAPTER 6

She-Do:

CONFESSIONS PART II (USHER) - STACIA'S STORY

Well, here we are. The chapter I really didn't want to write but had to. It is where I lay bare how I, too, gave in to insecurity, and frustration and pain, and had a full-blown relationship with another man. These are my confessions.

After learning of Ed's affair, there were days I was struggling to simply exist. In the fall, I was contacted by an old flame of mine, and I do mean flame. I had met this man, what seemed to be a hundred years ago, and instantly fell for him, though our relationship never made it to an official status. He was hilarious, talented, smart, and attentive. He had met my mom and sister, and mom thought he was the bee's knees. In the end, all we ever were then was a bit of a thing, but not an actual thing. One thing was true, though, there was always the need for an extinguisher when we were around each other.

So, getting back to the contact. The contact was simple. A "Hey, how are you doing, and I'll be in your city soon, maybe we can have dinner," message. Nothing inappropriate, I have dinner with lots of old friends, male and female. I was 100% sure I could have dinner with an ex-flame that never became even a flame as easily as I could with an ex-boyfriend without any concerns whatsoever. Except this circumstance was anything but normal and I should've been on high alert. First, if I'm being honest, this person was my kryptonite, especially physically. I knew that but pushed the thought out of mind. Secondly, I was in the midst of a marital crisis. This was a perfect storm, a backdraft type of fire, and I walked right into it.

We met for dinner and had the most amazing time laughing, reminiscing, and catching up on where we were in our lives. We were both married. We both had children and successful careers. We spent some time talking about why we didn't work, and what if we had? What if we still could? I realize how ridiculous that sounds - what if we still could? We were both married, how could that even be, but we did talk about it often during the course of our relationship. That night, I had parked at his hotel and we walked to dinner. Walking back to the hotel, I'd be lying if I said I didn't know the question of if I wanted to come up, wouldn't be asked. I started playing with fire that night and was quickly and easily consumed by the flames.

From that first reconnection visit onward, we talked on the phone almost daily, sometimes for hours. He was a phenomenal listener, always had my back, and gave me a lot of great advice about how to handle the current calamity that was my marriage. It may come as a shock to many, but because he cared about me, and wanted me to be happy, many times he would try and help me see Ed's point of view in our situation. He knew from our conversations that I still loved Ed very much and that I had a family I was trying to keep intact. However, these conversations also served to bring the two of us closer together. I was living two lives, one that was happy, and light and offered a strong physical connection, where I felt deeply desired, and one where I was struggling to see if I could bring any of that back.

We couldn't see each other often, as we never lived in the same city, but when we did, we would have a great time. Dinner, long conversations, always a lot of laughter, and physical intimacy. When I say that I feel like he understood me, and most importantly *saw* me, I mean it and that fueled our connection. He always paid such close attention to me. Details, like the time when he told me that I could stand behind a curtain with 10 other women and stick only our hands out and he would be able to instantly pick mine out of the lineup. He would spend time counting the beauty marks on my back. Over several years, he provided me with comfort, advice, friendship, love, and attention that I felt Ed struggled with even *before* we entered the rockiest part of our relationship.

During the time of this extramarital relationship, our family moved to Texas. Every move we'd made as a couple or as a family was precipitated by me; for me to go to graduate school, for my job promotions. For several winters in Indiana, Ed would get almost depressed (seasonal effectiveness disorder is real) and talk about moving to warmer temperatures. We loved our friends, our jobs, our house in Indiana and I, for one, was relishing in some stability for our kids and thought we wouldn't move again until after they had graduated from Carmel High School.

In December of 2010, we were standing with our family on the beach in Newport Beach, California wearing light sweaters and jeans. Ed looked at me and said, "*Please,* can we get out of the cold weather now? We could live like this (arms outstretched in front of the ocean for effect)!"

I recall saying to him, "We can't move the kids again," each time he mentioned moving to me before this and each time he would say, "Those kids will be fine, what about me?"

In hindsight, that was a profound missed signal on my part. He felt as if he had sacrificed his happiness, his desires, perhaps even taken a career back seat to mine and it was time for me to finally pay up. Well, I certainly didn't like living in the cold either, so I considered it a sign when we stepped off of the plane from California a few days later at the Indianapolis International Airport, the snow and wind was blowing so hard, it was snowing sideways! That was enough for me to say to him, "Okay, we'll create a list of cities to consider. Apply for interesting roles and whoever finds a job first, that's where we'll move."

The job searches began in earnest in January in our five named cities, Phoenix, San Diego, Raleigh/Durham or Charlotte, Atlanta; and our last-minute addition: Dallas. By February, there had been few nibbles for either of us which had us wondering if we had interpreted the signs correctly, maybe we weren't supposed to leave the Midwest just yet. Then came Superbowl weekend and I had a phone interview with a company in Dallas which, interestingly enough, is where the big game was being played that year. The city was blanketed in ice right before the game (that is a truly North Texas phenomenon, it doesn't happen often, but ice storms bring the entire area to a grinding halt), so the woman who would later become my supervisor was sharing with me how the conditions were so terrible, everyone was working from home and wondered aloud if I would be comfortable living in a city where this happened, albeit infrequently, because everything shut down and no one could drive. I chuckled, "I'm from Michigan. I know cold. I also know that *no one* can drive on ice!" After a great conversation about my experience in healthcare sales and marketing and my career aspirations, I was invited to Dallas to interview with a panel of additional people. It was Spring break time, so the interviews would have to take place in late March. After successfully interviewing with people that would be my colleagues and business partners, I was offered a position that was a promotion and the company would pay for our relocation. I was to start the day after Memorial Day and the family drove down with me to help me move into an apartment temporarily since we didn't know when Ed would move down. He was going to stay at his current employer until he had a job in Texas of course, and the kids would move down in the Summer and start school in Texas. Since getting married, even during the time when Ed stayed in a hotel at night, for a short period after I discovered his affair, we had *never* been apart for more than a few days. This physical separation was going to be indefinite and I would be lying if I didn't admit that I was a bit uneasy, especially after what we'd been through. Now our tenuous relationship was being put to another test and we would have to exercise our trust, in each other and in God, that things would be OK. Meanwhile, I hadn't at all severed ties with the other man in my life.

It happened that Ed was able to secure a position the week that they brought me to move in and I was so happy. I would only be alone for a few weeks and then he would be back to move in and start his job. We talked on the phone for hours every night about everything, how I was afraid I would be swept away in one of the magnificent tornadoes that happen in North Texas each Spring, logistics of the move, his going-away parties with friends, and how we were going to manage the kids getting to Texas after their Summer vacation with their Grandma Di. In six weeks, we were all reunited, the kids started at their new middle school where they played sports and made new friends. After a few months we were settling in nicely. Our jobs were going well, and we had found a church home we really liked and got involved in. The children were very involved in the middle school ministry and Ed and I worked with our Couples ministry. We were happy campers again. Or so it appeared.

Our church hosted, and still does, epic couples retreats. Since Ed and I served on the marriage ministry this annual retreat was always a busy time for us. During the second conference we were on the planning committee for, after hurriedly getting the venue set up, getting couples checked in and to their tables for the evening, we settled in to the open session. We enjoyed the worship music and the ice breakers, allowing us to get to know those at our table.

The opening message that night was from Pastor Eric Wooten, who I mentioned several chapters ago. The topic was the Anatomy of an Affair, recognizing the signs and so people could pull themselves out before going down the road to physical intimacy. It was so interesting because he used a real couple as an illustration of how this can happen. In this case, the wife had been unfaithful, and the video interviews were done with her "in shadow" as she discussed how she found herself on every step in the path, how easily she justified her actions, and how the emotional affair ultimately led to infidelity. It was painful, but efficient, as Pastor Eric laid out the path I was already at the end of and I heard God's voice say to me, "Stacia. You need to tell Ed. This is the exact path you've been on. You need to confess this to him. Tonight."

Of course, I tried to ignore it at first, but when the sermon ended, and they turned on the light during the last interview with the woman and revealed that it was the Pastor's wife, it hit me like a ton of bricks! It was so powerful. He (and she) were so brave, especially because y'all know how judgmental "church folk" can be; happy to point at your sin and shake their head, when they have messes of their own to clean up. They used themselves as an example of how easily this can happen *to anyone*, but also how a marriage could survive an affair.

There was a breakout session immediately after this discussion, as well as 20-minutes counseling sessions with the Pastor and his wife for which people could sign up. We signed up for a slot and then went outside to complete our breakout assignment. I heard the voice in my head again, "DO IT. Tonight you tell the truth."

There are two main reasons I didn't want to. Number one is obvious; I was afraid it would be the end of my marriage and I didn't want that. The second was the harder one to contend with. I was selfish, and I wasn't anywhere near ready for my other relationship to end. Because he had helped me so much, by being so emotionally available and supportive, he made me feel incredible about myself, like I was the prize. He had come back into my life after so long, and *right* as I had entered crisis mode, I had convinced myself that God was not only OK with it, but that He gave this relationship back to me because he knew I needed it.

Yikes! Scary to admit that but that is precisely how I felt, so I had a bit of a quick argument with my Heavenly Father about how he could give me such a good thing and then expect me to willingly let it go.

It was a quick argument, though, as the words repeated. "Tell him. Now." I honestly don't remember the words I said,

I'm sure Ed does, but I told him about the affair. I told him with whom (Ed knew this person was my kryptonite) and how long it lasted. I told him I would end it because I wanted him, our marriage, and our family. I was willing to accept his disappointment and anger with me, but I wanted to fight for our marriage. Now, my husband does not cry often and so I do vividly remember quiet tears streaming down his face. There was no yelling and screaming like when I discovered his affair. Just pain and I was responsible. He agreed to still keep our mini-counseling appointment in about 20 minutes and in that short period of time, Eric and his wife were able to get us both in alignment to fight to stay together.

We would continue with some private counseling with The Wooten's for a while and felt ourselves get back on track. We have only looked forward since then.

If it seems too good to be true, it probably is.

There were so many things I could've and should've done differently that it is hard to narrow in on one. One scripture, however, I think strikes to the heart of the issue, Jeremiah 17:9. I like the Contemporary English version whose translation says, "You people of Judah are so deceitful that you even fool yourselves, and you can't change," as I think it explains the deceit and the incurability of the human heart. The old adage, the heart wants what the heart wants, then takes on a new meaning - we shouldn't trust what the heart wants, it's deceitful! The Scripture also suggests that we, in our own power, have no hope in changing the heart, so we need the power of God to have any chance in doing so.

Be honest with yourself

As humans, especially women, we crave attention, to be desired, and to feel special and we equate that with love. I should've been honest with myself and Ed that I wasn't getting that need met instead of accepting it from someone else. I forgot (or more accurately, ignored) that God never brings chaos into a situation, and being involved with someone else, even if it 'felt' good, was chaos, and I couldn't help myself out of the pit of temptation once I'd jumped in headfirst.

CHAPTER 7

She-Do:

HEALING BEGINS (TENTH AVENUE NORTH)

Now you know. The entire ugly backstory. How could two people who fell so quickly and deeply in like and in love end up in swimming in a sea of infidelity? No doubt, some readers have twisted their lips up and declared, "mmmm hmmmmm, can't nobody be that happy! I knew all that glittered wasn't gold." You may even have repeated some of your own 'never' Capital "V" vows while reading our story. Well, that's none of our nevermind, you go right ahead if that makes you feel better about yourself. But read on if you want to hear how we continue to run this marriage race to see what the end is going to be! For me - the key lesson I learned was to...

Let (it) go!

Now, this was really, really, really hard for me, even though I had also been unfaithful, I blamed Ed for it. If I hadn't been hurt first, there is no way I would've cheated on him, right? I recall telling one of my absolute ride-or-die girlfriends, that even though I was 'happy' in my other relationship and as much as I always adored the other man that had come back into my life, I would give it all back to never have had Ed cheat on me. Well, since we can't rewrite history, we'll never know the answer to the question of if I wouldn't have succumbed to my desires but, I had to release Ed from the rage cage that I had put him in. I had to choose to trust him, not berate him about what he'd done. I could not allow myself to live in constant fear that it would happen again and again (the adage, once a cheater, always a cheater). I had to trust God and at the time, my trust with Him was shaky at best, I had to trust that somehow, someway, this situation would be used for my good (who loves him). I had to leave, correction, I had to truly *put* my marriage in his hands.

Fight to Fix—Not to Win

This principle is lifted directly from some of the teachings of our Couples Ministry. Of course, we still fight, albeit rarely. We are still two imperfect and selfish human beings, trying to replicate the perfection of God's unselfish love and this takes a lot of maturity and discipline! Instead of needing to be right, I have to remind myself that it is more important that the situation we are disagreeing about is righted. That I am stronger, bonded in love and fidelity to my husband than on my own and sometimes, winning a battle is not worth risking the foundation we've built to help us win the war. So, when I get hot headed, a great grounding scripture here is Romans 14:19, So then we pursue the things which make for peace and the building up of one another.

He-Do:

AFTER THE LOVE IS GONE (EARTH WIND & FIRE)

Following the aftermath of my confessions, began the darkest time for our marriage. I was officially put on the clock by Stacia to figure out (what I felt was single-handedly no less) what our fate was going to be, and I was going to have to prove and confirm what direction we were going in. I was going to have to show Stacia what steps I was going to take to never do this again and provide the assurances that I had truly learned my lesson. I remember thinking that what I heard in these conversations were directions about what _I was_ going to do and how _I needed_ to validate and prove my new commitment to saving our marriage. The pressure mounted as I figured I needed to be perfect in every way for her. I knew I had no room for error, and any missteps were going to be scrutinized to high heaven. Although she said she still loved me and her love for me was not gone, it sure felt like it!

And oh, after the love has gone

How could you lead me on

And not let me stay around?

Oh, after the love has gone

What used to be right is wrong

Can love that's lost be found?

[After the Love Has Gone, Earth Wind and Fire]

When all the dust cleared after the affair was uncovered and we began the long path to trying to heal, and even decide if we were going to make it, I needed to come to grips with just how broken I was. I had to force myself to look inward and accept that everything I thought I wasn't getting from Stacia was because I never once truly looked at it from her perspective. I had only been concerned about myself and how I felt, that it didn't become apparent to me until everything came out, this was all due to my selfishness and lack of emotional maturity that put me in this position. There was a period of time during some of our counseling that I felt so broken and sad, I could not even look at myself in the mirror. The very thought that I had brought all this pain and hurt into Stacia's world by my actions was sobering. I wasn't a great guy. I wasn't a great husband. And what example of a father was I leaving for my kids? It was a long and difficult journey for me to finally reach the stage of forgiveness with Stacia. Our success depended on my commitment to taking full responsibility for the betrayal, being patient and understanding that the healing process was a journey that I had to be willing to go on with her.

As we began to pick up the pieces and started to try to understand exactly where it all went wrong, for me specifically, I knew I had to focus on what love meant to me, and how I would go forward showing this in our relationship. We both made a commitment to leverage not only what we learned from counseling, but we also became purposeful in honing-in on sermons where the focus of the message was how to love one another as much as Christ loves us. This ultimately forced me to really examine what unconditional love truly meant and I was going to have to accept that love and sacrifice went together in a marriage. I focused so much on me and my needs I left out the most important person, and that was Stacia. In one of our Pastor's lessons on unconditional love, he highlighted that marriage was a complete acceptance of putting the other first. I had to let go of my ego and my need for feeling like the man was in conflict with what Jesus did for us every day which was to be in the moment and be willing to give selflessly. But let me tell you, to give in that manner and be willing to accept the end result no matter what, was so hard for me. My initial fear was that I was giving in way too much and I would be letting my wife own and control the relationship. I was afraid to trust in that unconditional love. But once I became obedient to His will and not mine, a funny thing happened, I felt good. All of a sudden, things began to turn around. Communication was easier in our relationship. The uneasiness and apprehension slowly went away between us dealing with the past and focused on the present and more about how much better we were going to be.

It was really about faith, believing that if I submitted to the relationship there would be some positive outcome for not only myself, but for Stacia as well. By me doing the right thing and allowing her to witness that I was going to be fully engaged, it freed her from the burden of worrying about what I was doing, if I was going to leave, step out on our marriage again, or if I truly loved her the way she desired to be loved. The hard work was just listening and trusting and allowing all that we were learning to be used in our relationship. When you think about it, as much wrong as we do, God / Jesus never leaves us and all He is doing is waiting for us to realize that, so we can see we are not alone. It doesn't mean life is perfect, and that there will never be struggles, but He's there to give us strength and fortitude that in the end He is still in control.

We both needed to be open to recreating our relationship and letting go of those areas that were not working. We were not going to be the same as before, but it was OK, because now we both had a vested interest in rebuilding and emerging with a better sense of who we are and what we wanted our marriage to be. It was going to be the hardest work that either of us could imagine but staying committed to it would be the thing that would save the marriage.

Deliverance is a verb

The process of healing from such hurt takes a considerable amount of patience and determination. Initially, we struggled to communicate without each conversation ending up with me apologizing and then Stacia unsure if she was ready to accept my apology (or lack of sincerity) because I should not have put her in the predicament in the first place. It only took a short amount of time before we knew that some form of counseling was going to be needed. We set out to have counseling help us with the ultimate decision of deciding if we were going to be able to stay with one another, or if we were so damaged that we would have to make the tough decision of divorcing. With so much uncertainty swirling around us, we forged ahead with the hopes that we would be able to get guidance and direction.

I was floored, I was hurt, but then again, I was not surprised. Here was the test. Was I going to run and give myself an out or was I going to show the ultimate love and sacrifice to my wife just as God had shown me?

I had been delivered and given a second chance, and now I could exhibit this same thing to my wife because I should be able to identify and relate to what she now felt. I knew I could make it because God had now put my heart and soul in a different position, and just like that, I could accept her admission and forgive her. If I didn't, I'm not sure we would have made it.

CHAPTER 8

We-Do:

YOU'RE STUCK WITH ME (TAMIA)

A portion of the lyrics of this song, by Canadian-born R&B star Tamia:

When I'm not with you

I feel lost without you

I'm telling the truth

I'm so lost without you

Baby you're stuck with me

After such devastation, you may be asking if it is at all possible to still feel this way? Well, in our case, the answer is yes! We are very much in love, still like each other a lot and enjoy each other's company. It is not a cakewalk though, and we have had to internalize and systematize some of our lessons in order to continue going strong and, since seven is the Biblical number of completion and perfection, here are seven of our major lessons.

One

GET help (Help! - The Beatles)

We have been to a few marriage counselors since that picture got smashed in our bedroom many years ago. During our sessions, we have learned how to articulate our needs to each other and about how our different personality styles contribute to how we read a situation, both positive and negative, and our reactions to it. Particularly, in times of disagreement, we have learned to take a moment to breathe, ask clarifying questions, and most importantly, to think that the other person has good intentions. It is amazing how people can change their point of view - by thinking the best of their spouse instead of thinking that they are trying to hurt them.

Help doesn't only come from a professional (though we still highly recommend that), but also by surrounding yourself with couples who exhibit healthy relationship habits as role models, who will hold you accountable to doing the same in your marriage, and who are willing to step in and help/pray at a moment's notice. It is so important to build these communities *before* you can imagine needing them. From watching our kids so we could have a peaceful screaming match at home, to offering a shoulder to cry on, we couldn't have stayed on this journey without our tribe of married friends. At our church in Texas, we have small groups that are composed of people in "like states"; married couples, singles, divorced individuals, seniors, etc. This has been important, to have a group of people that can pour into our relationship when needed and vice versa. Also, and this may sound harsh, but if you are a married man, why in the world would you seek advice from one of your single friends (and yes, you can replace man for woman)? They may be a close confidant, but they are not in the covenant that you are. They have the luxury of thinking about themselves first, second and third. Not having to put someone else's happiness above their own. Married men understand the sacrifice (remember talking about dying every day - LOL) needed to unconditionally love their wives. They can counsel each other about the right way to handle marriage stressors and what God has to say about it. We also still attend the Couples Conference at our church. Had we not been at the one in 2013, we may never have gotten to the point of full transparency and forgiveness.

Now, this most certainly does not mean that we don't continue to have disagreements, and sometimes fall back into poor communication patterns, and so that's why we have a Sunday evening calendar appointment to check-in with each other.

CREATE a plan (God's Plan - Drake)

"No discipline is enjoyable while it is happening - it's painful! But afterward, there will be a peaceful harvest of right living for those who are trained in this way," Hebrews 12:11 NLT. You see, we now understand that there were quite a few areas of our relationship with each other and our relationship with God that were not at all on solid ground. Our individual and collective relationship with the Lord was not first in our lives. Going to Him first, trusting Him and His Word instead of taking things into our own hands should have been what we did. Instead, we turned on each other and turned to other people to fill the void. This is the pride of man though, isn't it? We don't trust that God can handle our problems. We try to hide them from Him. And, unfortunately, no matter how many times that does *not* work, we keep doing it. We wish we could tell you we are 100% perfect in doing so now, but we aren't. We are so much better than we used to be, though, through creating our plan, based on who God says we are to be to each other, and it has proven to be the difference maker.

We try to have consistent date nights, but also weekly 'business meetings' which was really important when the kids were still living at home. It is during business meetings, we can talk about when the plumber is coming or, when our kids were younger, who was responsible for picking up our daughter from the basketball game on Friday. The reason it is important to have this time set apart from date time is so that you don't spend your date nights family action planning and, instead, really focused on connecting to each other!

Three

COMMIT to working it out (Work - Vivian Green)

Determine you are in this thing and there is no getting out! Once you are married, God sees you as one being. Just because our society allows divorce, God doesn't do divorce,

He's like, "Who are you now?" Of course, there are a few instances where divorce is really still an option, such as physical abuse, but just because you all don't like each other anymore or your husband is acting like a fool, as our Pastor always says, "You married him. He's your fool now!"

Learn to fight fair (attacking the source of conflict, not each other and learning the rules of the ring, how to have productive conflict) and that it is not our spouse's job to make us happy, that is not what they are designed for and is a set up for failure. We are to be fulfilled by God and God alone and when we put anything in the number one spot where God is supposed to be, it is only a matter of time before it all comes crashing down so he can remind us that he is the source of our contentment. Note: I didn't say happiness. No one has the right to be happy. Life comes with suffering, I mean, if Jesus suffered, what makes me (or you) think you are too good to suffer? He was betrayed, he was lied on, he was tempted. But he showed us what to do in each of those circumstances and that is to turn to the Heavenly Father and leverage your relationship with Him. Ask Him for help. Cry out and admit that you are in trouble and desperately need Him. Turn to His Word and seek lasting comfort.

Four

LISTEN & TALK to each other (Can We Talk - Tevin Campbell)

It is critical to always think THE BEST of your spouse. That thing they said, may have been unartful, it may have missed the mark, but their intention is not to hurt you.

One of the areas that still requires focus for us, is the ability to connect and be willing to engage with one another when the going gets tough, and even to remain consistent in connecting emotionally. Ed recounts that it was always a challenge for him to be willing to talk and explore all of Stacia's feelings during our in-depth discussions, especially one that he thought he was in trouble! The learning was that if he wasn't willing to think to himself on a daily basis, *how can I make my wife's life better*, and be willing to open up a dialogue about it, then he was doomed to repeat the same failures and their relationship would be forever impacted. For him, just as important as connecting with her, was also the willingness to sit in the valley with her and show her that he may not be able to resolve or remove the emotions she was experiencing, but he cared enough to walk with her and experience the moment with her.

It demonstrated to Stacia how Ed was willing to do something that was uncomfortable to him and that he was ready, willing and able to be her emotional ear and support, and not always a problem solver. It's like the scene in the movie "Lord of the Rings" where Samwise Gamgee told Frodo, "I can't carry it [the ring] for you, but I can carry you!"

BE obedient - even when you don't want to (Do the Right Thing - Redhead Kingpin and the FBI)

One self-inflicted wound that was a direct reason for Ed's infidelity, was the inability (and unwillingness) to climb the emotional wall that Stacia would erect during times of stress in our relationship. Why does God make so many men emotionally challenged when it comes to real empathy? There were times that he would literally rather walk on hot coals than to sit down and actually ask 'what's wrong?' He'd never learned the skills to deal with emotional difficulty, and while he'd heard so many times that God isn't a fan of divorce, so he'd have to figure it out, it was distressing to say the least.

Further, imagine how hard it was for Stacia when she realized that her knight in shining armor was on the other side of her emotional wall with a dumbfounded look on his face and trying to decide if he was even going to try to get over the wall or not. It was important during this time, though not necessarily planned, that we remained in the church (remember Stacia's story earlier in the book about having a bit of a tiff with God while sitting in the pews). We remained in the same home, except for a brief stint. We committed to regular marriage counseling, even though there were many days Stacia went kicking and screaming, proclaiming nothing was going to work and they were doomed. All that said, we were obedient to remaining "one flesh."

HAVE faith! (Faithfully - Journey)

Looking back at this time as we were heading down the road to recovery, we both had to deal with many emotions. Love, hate. Anxiety, Depression. Fear, Faith. At one point the level of guilt and remorse weighed so heavily on both of us, individually and collectively, that we nearly cried to on a nightly basis. There was also the feeling of vast helplessness because there was no possible way we could see our own way out of such a colossal mess. How could we ever truly reach one another and begin the healing process? The truth is, in our own power, we couldn't and as soon as we accepted that, things changed. We had to switch our mindsets and keep the endgame in mind. *Stay married, no matter what.*

Like any important moment in our lives when we really want something, like getting accepted to our number one college, getting that promotion at work, having kids; it is critical to move through the fear and face your challenges with the strength of Samson. We can see the most growth in ourselves when we are willing to face a challenge with the goal of progress vs. perfection and not obsessing about the how, and certainly not whether or not we will fail. A movie we both love, Red 2, has a line which speaks perfectly to this. It's the point when John Malkovich's character, Marvin, tells Bruce Willis' Frank Moses to "Make the run to emotional safety," if he really wants to experience happiness. You can reach bliss, but only if you are willing to run towards danger.

Seven

BELIEVE in your Love (ENDLESS LOVE - Lionel Richie & Diana Ross)

How do you get through all of the hurt and damage created by infidelity? Anchor yourself in prayer, accept God's forgiveness and BELIEVE!

It is important to remember that love isn't a feeling - it is an active choice we make each day. To stay in the work in order to reap the rewards, it's our strong advice to determine up front, there ain't no separating—believe! Get help if you need it. Commit to working it out. Listen and talk to each other and be obedient, even when you don't want to. The foundation of it all, HAVE FAITH!

Life will always test you to see if you are going to stick to your guns or if you are going to bail. Our goal in writing this book is to help other couples so that they never have to go through what we did. It was also created with several relationship dynamics in mind:

- o Couples who are struggling. May this help you to realize that there is always light at the end of darkness.
- o For couples who may not have made it through together. Perhaps you can be willing to give love and marriage another try one day.
- o For singles who want to build a solid foundation from the start of their future marriage.

Our sincere prayer is that you will identify weak spots in your relationship, *really* put God in the center and go to Him *first* for guidance, support and direction, so that you can say *We Re-Do* for a lifetime!

We believe we can do it. We believe you can too!

AFTERWARD

SO IN LOVE (JILL SCOTT FEAT. ANTHONY HAMILTON)

While reliving some of our darkest days in writing this book wasn't easy, we can honestly say that we now enjoy an even closer bond with one another, as impossible as that may seem. Through the many years that have passed since our world was shaken to its core, we have much more of an appreciation for one another, as well as for our individual needs and triggers so that we can stop any negative spiraling before it begins. With that comes a new-found strength and confidence that we can make it through anything.

The hardships that we experienced due to our infidelity showcases just how far left a marriage can go when there isn't meaningful and honest communication, which requires a lot of introspection by both partners, to uncover potential challenges. And having had to deal with the ramifications of not handling those challenges for so many years of our marriage, we never want to go down that path again! We understand more deeply now that marriage is more than a commitment, it is really a covenant, between us and God. He sees us as one and we have to be willing to give our best daily, without expecting anything in return.

The only competition that exists between us now, is in trying to best "serve" the other person. Being "other-focused" allows us to continue to fortify the foundation of love and respect that we've always had, through all of the *sadness* and the *madness*. We now *know that we know* that it is possible to have a successful marriage and rekindle a deep love, even after what would have destroyed many.

Since recovering from this pain, we have enjoyed the graduation of both of our kids from high school, one from college (the other in the Spring of 2021), trips to Hawaii and a bucket list trip to Australia. We have welcomed a few new babies into the family and celebrated the wedding of Stacia's cousin, Ryan (Megan). We have comforted each other through the horrendous losses of Ed's Mom, Stacia's Papa, Aunt, and Grammy, and know that we couldn't have made it through such pain without each other.

The journey we experienced also demonstrated that there is no magic bullet to healing from hurt and betrayal, rather we really had to do the hard work; be all in for the joy and pain. Most counseling professionals advise that when going through a relationship issue as painful as infidelity, the couple goes individually and collectively, through the classic stages of grief: Shock & Denial, Anger, Bargaining, Depression and finally, Acceptance. It is a loss. The loss of the relationship you thought you had. The one you dreamed of. It is a painstaking effort that requires time and a commitment to the covenant you've made. While it was not easy, we have been able to show that it is possible to reclaim the ability to live truthfully, to dig deep into unhealthy patterns that need to be severed and recover a healthy, fulfilling and loving marriage.

There is now beauty for the ashes that our relationship fell into. In a strange way, doing the work together and individually to recover from our affairs, allowed us to rediscover how to love each other, and ourselves even more deeply.

The soul searching that we each had to do, allowed us to forgive one another, and importantly, forgive ourselves for straying. Both of us have gained skills about how to protect the marriage by recognizing the triggers that led down dark paths and to stop the spiral before it starts. Now, the work never ends, it is a constant process of noticing when one of us feels off, unseen, or unheard and talking about how to remedy those emotions in a healthy, marriage edifying way. We are relishing in our rebirth and recommitment to each other, our increasing faith in God, and are so in love as the title of this chapter suggests, we no longer live in fear of violating our vows. What God has joined together, let no man (including us) put asunder.

Acknowledgements

We could not have moved forward on our journey to write this book without a lot of love, support and respect from our village! Maybe somewhat surprisingly, to them at least, we'd like to first thank our children, Chris and Alexa Gowens. Wanting, actually *needing*, to chart a positive course for you and show you what real love looks like gave us the courage to do the work. Wanting to interrupt the marital patterns we'd seen growing up was of paramount importance to both of us and We KNEW we had to not just stay together, but to find our way back to happiness!

Our families have always supported our relationship, even when some of them knew that something bad happened, but maybe not exactly sure what. The love that they have for us as individuals and as a unit was a warm blanket on cold nights. So, thanks mom, Diane, bonus dad, Bob, and mom, Carolyn–in heaven. dad-Ken and dad-Louis and stepmom Lynette; uncle Chuck and our sorely missed aunt Debbie; sisters Shannon, Lynda, Lisa, Leslie; brothers Louis, Lamar, Lael; cousins who double as siblings, Freda, Chad, Ryan and Meg, Courtney, Madison and Amanda. And to our grandparents, simply known as Grammy and Papa. You always treated Ed like a grandson, not by marriage, just your grandson, and we will be forever grateful that we were blessed with people who always believed we were best together!

Thank you to the friends that we had that supported us during the good times and bad. So many of our friends are more like family and we love them just as if they are! Special mention to Ryan and Dalana Brand, Kevin and Tasha White, Erin Ewens Brown, Stacia's sister, Shannon Charles, Stacia's cousins Alfreda Clark and Chad McMillan and finally, Stacia's Mom, retired Principal and English/Journalism teacher, Diane McMillan for reading this book in its various forms before it was ready for prime time. The feedback and editing assistance to make it much better is much appreciated. To our Indie Publisher, iWriteBooks' Myunique Green. She was professional, timely, inspirational and made this process so much easier for us.

To our "pre-launch" read and review crew, thank you for being willing to give the book its first official reviews that will, no doubt, identify reasons others should buy a copy! Please charge our heads, not our hearts, if we've neglected to mention anyone who has been an integral part of bringing this book to life. If you have enjoyed reading as well, please visit Amazon.com, search for We Re-Do and leave us a review; we'd love to hear what you think.

Thank you to One Community Church and the Couples Ministry for creating environments and content that allowed us to start the long road to recovery or marriage. A special shout out to Eric and Jill Wooten. Without their courage to share their "way back" during that couple's conference of 2013, that was most certainly orchestrated by God, we never would've found the courage to be honest, and begin the process of healing, leaning on the Lord, and recommitting to our endless love.

 Be blessed.

Discussion Questions

It is important to create an open dialogue with your spouse and we believe that the questions below, which are aligned with our seven major lessons learned: Get Help, Create a Plan, Commit to working it out, Listen & Talk to each other, Be Obedient, Have faith, Believe in your love, will serve as a guide to open up, get real, and have you exclaiming: We Re-Do!

Be sure each of you has something to write or type with to record your answers for further discussion.

Come and Talk to Me (Jodeci)

1) What are your thoughts on healthy couple communication? What does it look like for your marriage?
2) How do you secure the time to connect and communicate one-on-one as a couple? (i.e: without children)
3) What steps have you put in place to ensure you are actively listening (for understanding) rather than listening to respond when your partner is communicating with you?
4) Women: how do you regularly communicate to your husband that he is respected?
5) Men: how do you regularly communicate that she is loved?

The Matrimony (Wale featuring Usher)

1) Would you agree with this statement: My spouse is my biggest cheerleader? Discuss why you do or do not agree.
2) Do you both strive to love your spouse unconditionally–without an expectation of being "paid back"?
3) What role do you feel your faith plays in maintaining a healthy marriage? Is there alignment between the two of you?
4) Do you believe it's your spouse's job to make you happy?

Can you Stand the Rain (New Edition)

1) What Capital "V" vows have you made to yourself? Discuss them with your spouse.
2) How do you collaborate and discuss making big life changes such as job promotions, moves, having children, etc.?
3) Have you participated in couple's counseling? If not, discuss why. If you have, what benefits would you cite, and do you have a plan to continue counseling?

Steady Love (India Arie)

1) What are the top 10 things you need from your partner to be secure in your relationship?
2) How comfortable are you in operating in your partner's love language? Do you admit when you need help in this area?
3) Have you identified a successful marriage mentor tribe? If not, discuss who should be in your tribe.

Chances (Issac Caree)

1) Have either of you ever stepped foot on the 9 Steps to Affair we talked about in Chapter 3. If not, what has kept you from it? If so, how did you identify the inappropriate behavior and get off the path?
2) Is there anything in your marriage that you have not forgiven each other for?
3) How do you believe you could forgive each other, or forgive yourself, for breaking a vow made before God?

Made in the USA
Coppell, TX
25 November 2022

87037064R00066